SPELLING AND VOCABULARY WORKBOOK

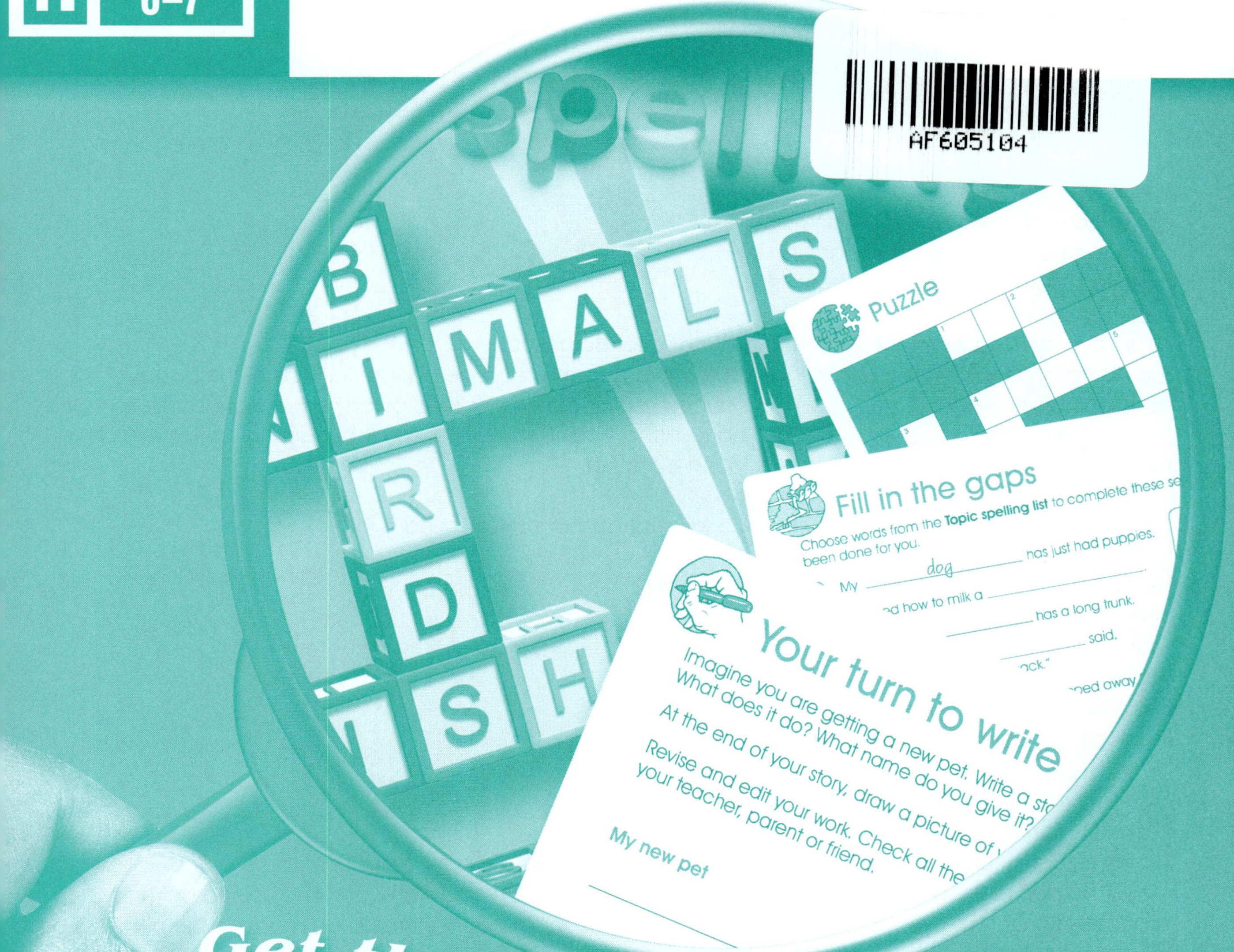

Get the Results You Want!

Donna Gibbs

Reprinted 2015, 2016, 2017, 2019, 2020, 2021, 2022

ISBN 978 1 74125 464 8

Pascal Press
PO Box 250
Glebe NSW 2037
(02) 8585 4050
www.pascalpress.com.au

Publisher: Vivienne Joannou
Series developer: Kristine Brown
Project editors: Mark Dixon and Leanne Poll
Edited by Leanne Howard
Reviewed by Dale Little
Typeset by Grizzly Graphics (Leanne Richters)
Cover and page design by DiZign Pty Ltd
Printed by Vivar Printing/Green Giant Press

Contents

Map of the book . . . . . Inside front cover
To the student iv
LOOK-SAY-COVER-WRITE-SAY-CHECK method 1

1 Looking at animals 2
2 At the beach 8
3 Sporting fun 14
4 At home 20
5 What's on the menu? 26
Review 1: Tests 1–6 32

6 Myself 36
7 Families 42
8 What are you wearing? 48
9 How many are there? 54
10 Moving around 60
Review 2: Tests 1–6 66

11 What season is it? 70
12 Where is it? 76
13 How does my garden grow? 82
14 Making sounds 88
15 Flying things 94
Review 3: Tests 1–6 100

Word list 104
Answers 106

To the student

Winnie the Pooh thought he was a good speller. It was just that some of the letters got out of order! The problem is that to be a good speller, all letters have to be in the correct order.

You can learn to be a good speller. There are rules for spelling words and there are spelling patterns that match sound patterns. This book will show you some of those patterns and teach you some of those rules. It will even teach you clever tricks to help you remember long words and words that don't fit the rules.

You will need a dictionary (the *Macquarie Junior Dictionary* if possible) and a sharp pencil. You will also need a quiet place to work with good light so you don't strain your eyes. You will be able to do the exercises in this book all by yourself if you have all those things.

It will also be a big help if you have an adult or big brother or sister to hear you spell the words once you think you know them. When you spell a word aloud to someone else, it stays in your brain much longer than if you just spell it to yourself.

You can't write well without good spelling. When you have finished this book, you will be well on the way to becoming a good writer.

You'll also find fun puzzles using the words from each unit. There are crosswords, wordsearches and other word games. There are jokes and riddles at the end of each unit that use the words you are learning.

I hope you enjoy working through the book. Good luck and have fun!

Q What's a magician's favourite subject?

A Spelling!

LOOK-SAY-COVER-WRITE-SAY-CHECK method

The **LOOK-SAY-COVER-WRITE-SAY-CHECK** method is always useful for learning to spell words. Follow these steps:

- **LOOK** at the word.
  What does it mean? What shapes do the letters make? What other words is it spelt like? Underline any hard parts.
- **SAY** the word aloud.
  Listen to the sounds in the word. Clap out its syllables. Spell it.
- **COVER** the word.
  Get ready to write it down.
- **WRITE** the word without looking back at it.
- **SAY** the word out loud again to check that you have remembered its sounds and spelling correctly.
- **CHECK** that the spelling is correct.
  If you get it right, write it once more. If you get it wrong, use the **LOOK-SAY-COVER-WRITE-SAY-CHECK method** again.

1 Looking at animals

Quick fun

Fill in the missing letters to spell the words from the box.
The first one has been done for you.

ant	bat
cat	duck
hen	lion

1. c a t
2. a _ _
3. h _ _
4. l _ _ _
5. d _ _ _
6. b _ _

Topic spelling list

Use the **LOOK-SAY-COVER-WRITE-SAY-CHECK** strategy to learn these words.

cat	dog	hen
duck	fox	chicken
ant	fly	bat
cow	kangaroo	lion
tiger	elephant	animal

Use this space to write out your topic words the first time. Use your own paper for extra practice.

Rewrite here those you had the most trouble with.

Spelling strategy

LOOK-SAY-COVER-WRITE-SAY-CHECK method

The **LOOK-SAY-COVER-WRITE-SAY-CHECK** method is always useful for learning to spell words. (You can check this out on page 1.) Follow these steps:

1. **LOOK** at the word.
2. **SAY** the word and listen to its sounds.
3. **COVER** the word.
4. **WRITE** the word.
5. **SAY** the word and listen to its sounds again.
6. **CHECK** that the spelling is correct.

Choose six of the most challenging words from the **Topic Spelling list** and write them in Column 1 below. Then use the LOOK-SAY-COVER-WRITE-SAY-CHECK method to learn and practise their spellings.

1				
2				
3				
4				
5				
6				

Fill in the gaps

Choose words from the **Topic spelling list** to complete these sentences. The first one has been done for you.

1. My ___dog___ has just had puppies.
2. I learned how to milk a ______________.
3. The ______________ has a long trunk.
4. The mother ______________ said, "Quack, quack, quack, quack."
5. The ______________ hopped away from us.
6. A ______________ hangs upside down to sleep.

Tricky words

The words ***lion*** and ***line*** sound the same but have different spellings. Think of a way to remember the difference.
For example: a *l**io**n* opens his mouth like an ***o***.

Word	Meaning	Example
lion	an animal from the cat family	*We saw a **lion** at the zoo.*
line	a long, thin mark	*He wrote his answer on the **line**.*

Complete the sentences with the correct word (*lion* or *line*).

1. She wrote the word on the ________________________.
2. The ________________________ in the zoo looked hungry.
3. I saw a ________________________ at the circus.
4. The teacher told us to rule a ________________________.

Looking at … rhyme

Words ending with the same sounds make **rhymes**.
For example: ***cat*** rhymes with ***bat***.

1. Add rhyming words from the box to this poem. The first one has been done for you.

duck fox pig rat

If I had a ______rat______
I'd not be fond of that.

If I had a ________________________
I wouldn't do a jig.

I think I'd like a ________________________
but it might chew my socks.

I'll settle for a ________________________
and hope it brings good luck.

2. Which animal from the **Topic spelling list** rhymes with these words?

a pen ________________________

b how ________________________

c bog ________________________

d pie ________________________

e pant ________________________

Proofreading

Find five spelling mistakes and write the words correctly below. The first one has been done for you.

Noah made a big boat for the animles. They came up the steps into his boat.

First came the lyons, then the tiggers. Then two kangeroos jumped up the steps.

It took the elefants a long time. Now they were all safe and dry.

1 animals

2 ____________

3 ____________

4 ____________

5 ____________

Vocabulary power

Animal babies have their own names.
For example: a baby ***cat*** is called a ***kitten***.

Match the adults with their babies in the lists below. The first one has been done for you.

Adult animal	Baby animal
1 bear	kid
2 dog	joey
3 chicken	pup
4 duck	cub
5 goat	duckling
6 kangaroo	chick

Read and learn

Read the text below. What do the words in **bold** mean?

We went to the dog pound so I could **choose** my new pet. I wanted a **stray** dog so I could give it a home. The dog I liked **best** was **mainly** brown. He looked cheeky but **friendly**. We liked each other at once.

Circle the answer closest in meaning to the word in **bold**. The first one has been done for you.

1	**choose**	a pick	b follow	c feed
2	**stray**	a big	b grey	c homeless
3	**best**	a good	b least	c most
4	**mainly**	a soon	b mostly	c shortly
5	**friendly**	a hot	b kind	c busy

Puzzle

Which animal is this? Choose each animal's name and write it in the box under its picture.

hen	dog	cat	bat	kookaburra
fox	duck	koala	pig	chick

1 ______ 2 ______ 3 ______ 4 ______ 5 ______

6 ______ 7 ______ 8 ______ 9 ______ 10 ______

Your turn to write

Imagine you are getting a new pet. Write a story about it. What does it look like? What does it do? What name do you give it?

At the end of your story, draw a picture of your new pet.

Revise and edit your work. Check all the punctuation and spelling. Make a published copy for your teacher, parent or friend.

My new pet

Reading for fun

✦ **What did the doctor say to the pony with a sore throat?**
❖ Don't worry. You're just a little hoarse.

✦ **What do polar bears eat for breakfast?**
❖ Snow flakes.

✦ **What do you call a fish with no eyes?**
❖ A fsh.

☞ Answers on page 106

2 At the beach

Quick fun

Unscramble the letters to make the words in the box. The first one has been done for you.

sun	sand
sea	waves
crabs	shell

1. ase sea
2. llehs ____________
3. nus ____________
4. vesaw ____________
5. rcbas ____________
6. ands ____________

Topic spelling list

Use the **LOOK-SAY-COVER-WRITE-SAY-CHECK** strategy to learn these words.

sun	sunny	swim
crab	fish	water
boat	rocks	towel
sunscreen	starfish	beach
ocean	sea	sand
waves	shell	octopus

Use this space to write out your topic words the first time. Use your own paper for extra practice.

Rewrite here those you had the most trouble with.

Spelling strategy

LOOK-SAY-COVER-WRITE-SAY-CHECK method

Choose six of the most challenging words from the **Topic Spelling list** and write them in Column 1 below. Then use the LOOK-SAY-COVER-WRITE-SAY-CHECK method to learn and practise their spellings.

1				
2				
3				
4				
5				
6				

Fill in the gaps

Choose words from the **Topic spelling list** to complete these sentences. The first one has been done for you.

1. We love going to the ____beach____ for a holiday.
2. I saw a ____________ scuttle under the rocks.
3. Dad forgot to take his ____________ and ____________ to the beach.
4. Some huge ____________ crashed over our boat.
5. The sun made the ____________ very hot.
6. A school of ____________ swam past us.

Tricky words

The words ***sea*** and ***see*** sound the same but have different spellings. Think of a way to remember the difference. Two more words like *sea* that have ***ea*** spellings are ***ocean*** and ***beach***—words describing water.

Word	Meaning	Example
sea	water that covers most of the earth	*I love to swim in the* ***sea****.*
see	using your eyes	*I can* ***see*** *a fish.*

1. Here are five more words with an ***ea*** spelling. Underline the ***ea*** in each word and then say the word aloud.
   - a near
   - b speak
   - c bread
   - d seat
   - e wear

2. Does the ***ea*** make the same sound in these words?

   Answer: ______________________

Looking at … syllables

A **syllable** is a unit of sound within a word. One syllable makes one beat. You can clap the beats to find how many there are in a word.

For example:

The words ***sand***, ***sea*** and ***fish*** get one clap each. They are **one**-syllable words.
The words ***sunny***, ***sunscreen*** and ***water*** get two claps each. They are **two**-syllable words.
Three claps make **three** syllables, and so on.

How many syllables does each word have? The first one has been done for you.

	Word	How many syllables?
1	beach	one
2	starfish	
3	boat	
4	rocks	
5	ocean	
6	octopus	
7	shell	

Proofreading

Find five spelling mistakes and write the words correctly below. The first one has been done for you.

It is sumer at last. I am going to have my first swim tooday.

I have put a towle, my swimmers and some sunscrean in my beech bag.

1. summer
2. ______
3. ______
4. ______
5. ______

Vocabulary power

Many words are made by adding two words together.
The new word is called a **compound word**.
For example: ***star*** + ***fish*** makes ***starfish***.

Which two words are these compound words made from?
The first one has been done for you.

1. seashell sea + shell
2. sunscreen ______ + ______
3. shellfish ______ + ______
4. seagull ______ + ______
5. jellyfish ______ + ______
6. bluebottle ______ + ______
7. swimsuit ______ + ______
8. sandcastle ______ + ______

Read and learn

Read the text below. What do the words in **bold** mean?

I go to swimming lessons on Monday.
There are four **other** children in my class.
We wear goggles to **protect** our eyes.
I can dog paddle a **short** way now.
I need to **improve** much more. One day I
hope I can swim so **fast** that I'll win a race.

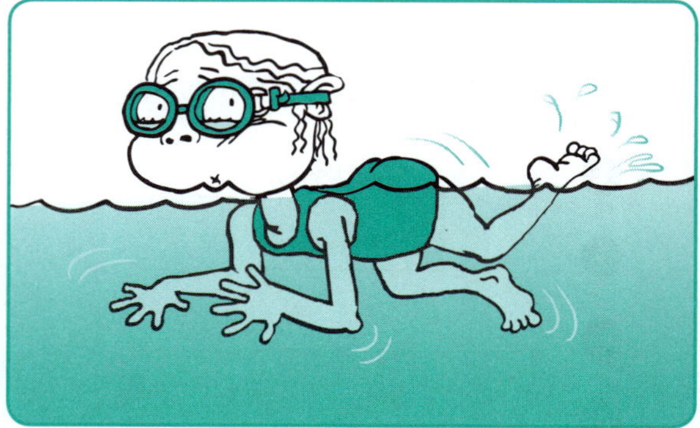

Circle the answer closest in meaning to the word in **bold**. The first one has been done for you.

1 **other**	a little	b more (circled)	c different
2 **protect**	a watch	b keep safe	c worry
3 **short**	a little	b lengthy	c far
4 **improve**	a get worse	b sharpen	c get better
5 **fast**	a slowly	b softly	c quickly

Puzzle

Find these words in the wordsearch puzzle below. Words go across and down.

sea	heat	shell	goggles
swim	water	sand	pool

s	e	a	b	h	p	r	g
h	e	a	t	q	o	m	o
e	v	s	l	w	o	d	g
l	s	w	i	m	l	u	g
l	i	a	n	s	t	a	l
b	u	t	t	a	r	m	e
f	g	e	o	n	e	c	s
p	t	r	o	d	o	i	l

Your turn to write

You are at the beach with your family. Your mother calls out, "Oh no! I've lost my watch." Tell what happens after that. At the end of your story, draw a picture.

Revise and edit your work. Check all the punctuation and spelling. Make a published copy for your teacher, parent or friend.

When Mum lost her watch

Reading for fun

✦ **Why do fish swim in salt water?**
❖ Because pepper makes them sneeze.

✦ **Why didn't the shrimp have any friends?**
❖ Because he was a bit shellfish.

✦ **How does the ocean say goodbye?**
❖ It waves.

☞ Answers on page 106

3 Sporting fun

Quick fun

These words have lost their first letter. Use the words in the box to find it. The first one has been done for you.

jump	hop
skip	ball
run	bounce

1. __r__ un
2. ___kip
3. ___all
4. ___ounce
5. ___ump
6. ___op

Use this space to write out your topic words the first time. Use your own paper for extra practice.

Topic spelling list

Use the **LOOK-SAY-COVER-WRITE-SAY-CHECK** strategy to learn these words.

run	ran	hop
jump	turn	skip
ball	bat	oval
beat	catch	match
bend	bounce	team
won	goal	race

Rewrite here those you had the most trouble with.

Spelling strategy

Little words in big words

Some words have other words hidden inside them.
For example: ***ball*** has the word ***all*** inside it. This can help you remember its spelling.

Find a little word hidden inside these words. The first one has been done for you.

1. bend ______end______
2. catch ____________
3. goal ____________
4. bounce ____________
5. race ____________
6. ran ____________

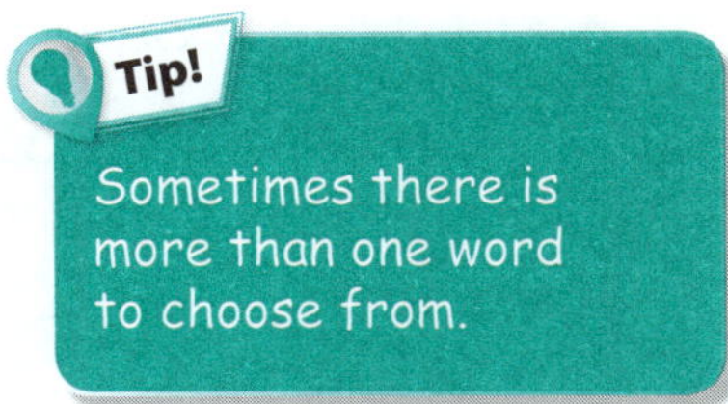

Fill in the gaps

Choose words from the **Topic spelling list** to complete these sentences. The first one has been done for you.

1. He kicked the ball and scored a ______goal______.
2. I'll ____________ you to the tuck shop.
3. He came first and ____________ a prize.
4. In gym we ____________ to touch our toes.
5. I play football on the ____________ on Fridays.
6. ____________ me if you can!

Tricky words

Some words are spelt and sound the same, but have different meanings.
For example: the word ***bat*** (something you use to hit a ball) and ***bat*** (a small animal with fur and wings).

Find the word from the **Topic spelling list** that has these different meanings.

1. **a** a game between people

   b thin bit of wood with an end that can be lit

   c exactly the same as something

   The word is: ______________________

2. **a** leave out

   b hopping from one foot to the other

   c a large open container

   The word is: ______________________

Looking at … word families

Word families are groups of words with a common base. Adding different letters changes the meaning of the word.

For example, here are some words that belong to the ***an*** family:
*b**an**, c**an**, f**an**, m**an**, n**an**, p**an**, pl**an**, r**an**, th**an**, v**an**.*

List some words that belong to the **op** (as in *h**op***) family.

1	6
2	7
3	8
4	9
5	10

Proofreading

Find five spelling mistakes and write the words correctly below. The first one has been done for you.

At our last criket game I made a duk. I want to make a better score in the matsh today.

I hit the ball hard. It flew up and across the ofal. A boy in the field ran towards it.

Would he catsh it? He did. Another duck!

1 cricket

2 

3 

4 

5 

Vocabulary power

Adverbs can tell how things are done. For example: *ran* ***quickly***, *bent* ***slowly***. They often end in ***ly***.

Choose an adverb from the box to add to these sentences. The first one has been done for you.

slowly	happily	angrily	quickly	loudly

1 The girls skipped happily in the sunshine.

2 My friend can swim much more __________ than I can.

3 The crowd shouted __________ at their team.

4 The coach spoke __________ because he was very cross.

5 The football bounced __________ towards the goal posts.

Read and learn

Read the text below. What do the words in **bold** mean?

My cousin has to **train** very hard at swimming. Every day she swims up and down the **lanes** in the pool. Her **coach** says she can swim really **quickly** now. One day, **perhaps**, she might swim at the Olympic Games.

Circle the answer closest in meaning to the word in **bold**. The first one has been done for you.

		a	b	c
1	**train**	try	dog paddle	practise (circled)
2	**lanes**	roads	spaces marked in the pool	expressway
3	**coach**	large bus	friend	trainer
4	**quickly**	fast	well	smoothly
5	**perhaps**	maybe	definitely	for certain

Puzzle

Draw pictures of three words of your choice from the list below. Label your drawings.

running hopping skateboarding swimming diving catching

Your turn to write

Write about an exciting race you have watched. Choose a title. Tell who took part, who watched and what happened. What made it exciting? Who won? At the end of your story, draw a picture of the race.

Revise and edit your work. Check all the punctuation and spelling. Make a published copy for your teacher, parent or friend.

Title ______________________________

____

____

____

____

____

____

____

____

Reading for fun

✦ **Why didn't Cinderella make the basketball team?**

❖ She ran away from the ball.

✦ **What lights up a soccer stadium?**

❖ A soccer match.

✦ **What goes up and down but does not move?**

❖ Stairs.

☞ Answers on pages 106–107

4 At home

Quick fun

Unscramble the letters to make the words in the box.
The first one has been done for you.

bedroom	stove
food	chair
plate	kitchen

1. fdoo ______food______
2. raich ________________
3. vtseo ________________
4. chtikne ________________
5. tlpae ________________
6. debmoor ________________

Topic spelling list

Use the **LOOK-SAY-COVER-WRITE-SAY-CHECK** strategy to learn these words.

bedroom	bathroom	kitchen
stairs	table	chair
cup	plate	food
stove	fridge	bench
box	garden	road
fence	gate	path

Use this space to write out your topic words the first time. Use your own paper for extra practice.

Rewrite here those you had the most trouble with.

Spelling strategy

Word shapes

Thinking about the **shape** of a word can help you remember its spelling. Look at the pattern made by letters going above, below or on the line. For example, here is the word ***food***:

1. Fill in the boxes with the word ***path***.

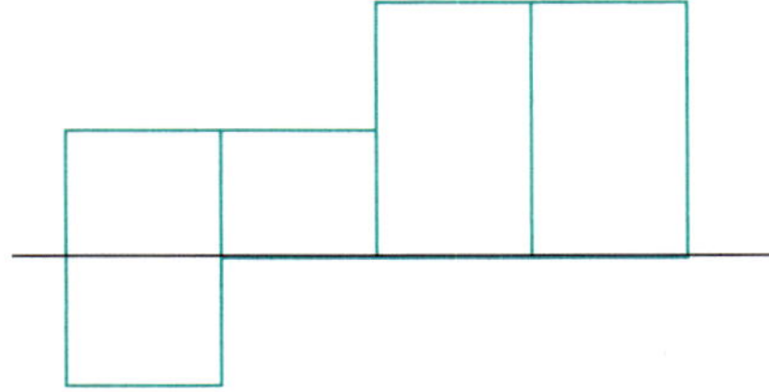

2. Fill in the boxes with the word ***kitchen***.

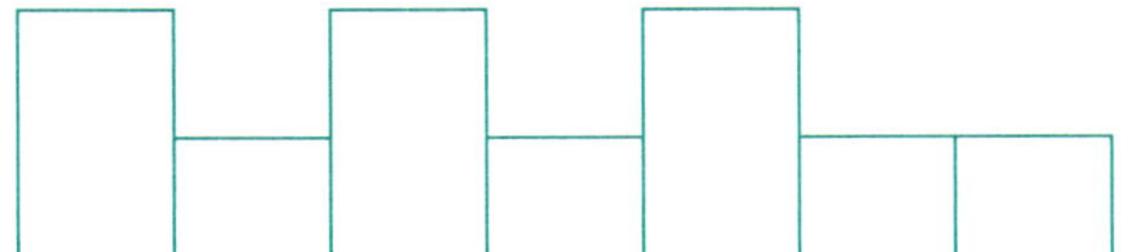

3. Fill in the boxes with the word ***table***.

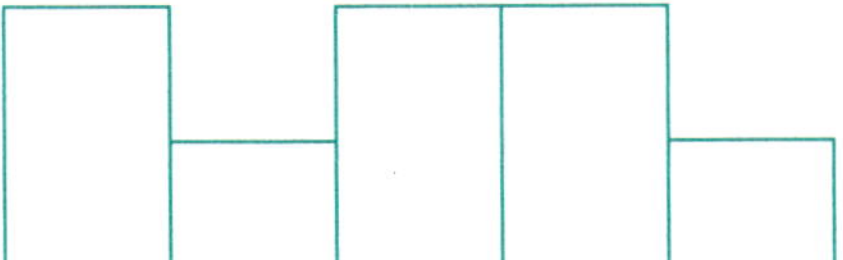

Fill in the gaps

Choose words from the **Topic spelling list** to complete these sentences. The first one has been done for you.

1. I have bunks in my ______bedroom______.
2. My job is to set the ____________________.
3. We grow beans in our ____________________.
4. My friend and I climbed up the ____________________.
5. Did you close the ____________________ to keep the dog in the yard?
6. We keep our milk in the ____________________.

Tricky words

The words ***stairs*** and ***stares*** sound the same but have different spellings. Think of a way to remember the difference.

For example: the space under a ***stair*** is filled with ***air***.

Word	Meaning	Example
stairs	steps that come one after another	*I climbed the **stairs**.*
stares	looks for a long time	*She is rude because she **stares** at me.*

Complete the sentence with the correct word—*stair*(*s*) or *stare*(*s*).

1. Don't ____________________ because it is rude.
2. I like to sit halfway down the ____________________.
3. If you ____________________ she will get cross.
4. Go down the ____________________ to the playroom.
5. "He's a ____________________ bear!"

Looking at … plurals

Most **plurals** (i.e. when there is more than one) are made by adding ***s***.

For example: *one **chair** → two **chairs***.

Sometimes a plural is made by adding **es** to a word. This happens after words ending with the letters ***s***, ***x***, ***z***, ***ch*** or ***sh***. It adds a syllable and makes the word easier to say.

For example: *one **dish** → two **dishes***.

Write the plurals of these words by adding **s** or **es**. The first one has been done for you.

1. one cup, ten cups
2. one bedroom, three ____________________
3. one stove, four ____________________
4. one bench, two ____________________
5. one path, six ____________________
6. one box, five ____________________

Proofreading

Find five spelling mistakes. Write the words correctly below. The first one has been done for you.

We moved into our new home today. Mum and Dad are unpacking boxs in the kitshen. My bedrume is much bigger than my old one. The gardenn is bigger too. I can see a boy near his gate across the rode. He might come to play.

1. boxes
2. __________
3. __________
4. __________
5. __________

Vocabulary power

Remember that **compound words** are made by adding two simple words together.

For example: the word ***bed*** when added to ***room*** makes ***bedroom***.

Which two words are these compound words made from? The first one has been done for you.

1. bathroom — bath + room
2. dishcloth — ________ + ________
3. inside — ________ + ________
4. outside — ________ + ________
5. playroom — ________ + ________
6. teapot — ________ + ________
7. homemade — ________ + ________
8. dishwasher — ________ + ________

Read and learn

Read the text below. What do the words in **bold** mean?

Mum and Dad have **agreed** to let me put up posters. It is hard to **decide** which posters to use. I also want to put up a calendar. Then I can **tick** off the days as they **pass**. I'd like my room to have bright colours so it looks **cheerful**.

Circle the answer closest in meaning to the word in **bold**. The first one has been done for you.

	a	b	c
1 **agreed**	forgot	said no to	said yes to (circled)
2 **decide**	choose	prefer	end
3 **tick**	write	mark	correct
4 **pass**	follow	go by	leave
5 **cheerful**	happy	cross	full of sun

Puzzle

Can you make at least six words out of the letters in the word ***bedroom***? The first one has been done for you.

1 bed

2 __________

3 __________

4 __________

5 __________

6 __________

Your turn to write

Write a description of your bedroom. What does it look like? What colours does it have? What is in it? Do you share it with someone? At the end of your description, draw a picture of your bedroom.

Revise and edit your work. Check all the punctuation and spelling. Make a published copy for your teacher, parent or friend.

My bedroom

Reading for fun

Knock, knock.

Who's there?

Doris.

Doris who?

Doris locked. That's why I knocked.

✦ **What gets wetter the more it dries?**
❖ A towel.

✦ **What room has no walls?**
❖ A mushroom.

✦ **What did one wall say to the other wall?**
❖ I'll meet you at the corner.

☞ Answers on page 107

5 What's on the menu?

Quick fun

Write the words from the box in alphabetical order. The first one has been done for you.

orange	pear
apple	butter
eggs	milk

1. apple
2. ______________
3. ______________

4. ______________
5. ______________

6. ______________

Topic spelling list

Use the **LOOK-SAY-COVER-WRITE-SAY-CHECK** strategy to learn these words.

apple	milk	banana
pear	orange	meat
lunch	breakfast	dinner
bread	butter	cheese
beans	peas	jam
honey	eggs	tea

Use this space to write out your topic words the first time. Use your own paper for extra practice.

Rewrite here those you had the most trouble with.

Spelling strategy

Learn a spelling rule: *ea* words

When **e** and ***a*** are next to each other in a word, the **e** comes before the ***a***.
For example: *s**ea**t*.

Find seven words with ***ea*** in them from the **Topic spelling list**. The first one has been done for you.

1. pear
2. ______
3. ______
4. ______
5. ______
6. ______
7. ______

Fill in the gaps

Choose words from the **Topic spelling list** to complete these sentences. The first one has been done for you.

1. Yum! Strawberry jam for my toast.
2. My dog slid on a ______ peel!
3. "I do like a little bit of ______ for my bread," said the King.
4. We had ham and ______ for breakfast.
5. Pooh Bear likes to eat ______ from the beehive.
6. I picked an ______ from our apple tree.

Tricky words

The words ***pear*** and ***pair*** sound the same but have different spellings. Think of your own way to remember the difference.

For example: inside a ***pair*** of shoes you'll find ***air***.

Word	Meaning	Example
pear	a brown or yellow fruit	*That* ***pear*** *came from this* ***pear*** *tree.*
pair	two of a kind	*I have a new* ***pair*** *of shoes.*

Complete the sentence with the correct word (*pear* or *pair*).

1. We added a ______________________ to the fruit salad.
2. I like having a ______________________ with ice cream.
3. On cold days, I wear a ______________________ of warm socks.
4. Could you lend me a ______________________ of gloves, please?

Looking at … vowels

There are five letters in the alphabet called vowels: ***a***, ***e***, ***i***, ***o*** and ***u***. Think of a way to remember them.

For example: the sentence ***A****nn's* ***E****gg* ***I****s* ***O****n* ***U****s*.

There are short vowels and long vowels. Vowels that make a short sound (e.g. ***a*** as in *c****a****t*) are called short vowels. Vowels that make a long sound (e.g. ***a*** as in *c****a****ke*) are called long vowels.

Sound out these words in front of a mirror. Are the **bold** vowels short or long? The first one has been done for you.

1. j**a**m ______short______
2. b**a**ke ______________________
3. pl**a**te ______________________
4. l**a**mb ______________________
5. t**a**ble ______________________
6. h**a**m ______________________

Proofreading

Find five spelling mistakes and write the words correctly below. The first one has been done for you.

Our famly likes lots of foods. Mum and Dad like meet and chese.

I like most things but I don't like benanas. My brother detests pairs.

Mum says he has to eat them.

1 family

2 

3 

4 

5 

Vocabulary power

Look at these three words—***little***, ***small***, ***tiny***. They all describe a kind of size. They are close in meaning to each other. Words close in meaning are called **synonyms**. They can make writing more interesting.

Which words in the box are synonyms for ***eat***? The first one has been done for you.

bite	dribble	gobble	chat	say
chew	let	munch	nibble	talk

1 bite

2 ____________

3 ____________

4 ____________

5 ____________

Read and learn

Read the text below. What do the words in **bold** mean?

Our teacher at school **taught** us how to make fruit salad. We **sliced** some **ripe** fruit into small pieces and mixed them all together. I am going to ask if I can make some **after** dinner tonight. Mum will be **surprised**!

Circle the answer closest in meaning to the word in **bold**. The first one has been done for you.

1	**taught**	a made	b showed	c asked
2	**sliced**	a cut	b jumbled	c mashed
3	**ripe**	a raw	b old	c ready to be eaten
4	**after**	a before	b during	c later than
5	**surprised**	a shocked	b amazed	c horrified

Puzzle

Solve this crossword puzzle by adding the missing words.

ACROSS

2 We eat ______ at school.

4 I like ______ with my cereal.

7 __________ is the first meal of the day.

DOWN

1 We have dessert after _______.

3 Milk can be made into butter and ________.

5 We picked green _____ from the vegie garden.

6 Mum drinks ____ from her tea cup.

Your turn to write

Make up a lunch menu you would like to find in a café. Add four meals and three drinks to choose from. Add pictures or patterns to decorate your menu.

Revise and edit your work when you have finished. Check all the punctuation and spelling.

Menu

Price:

Meals:

Drinks:

Reading for fun

Knock, knock.

Who's there?

Lettuce.

Lettuce who?

Lettuce in and we'll tell you!

- What word does ***stressed*** spell backwards?

 ____

- **What starts with *t*, ends with *t* and is filled with *t*??**

 A teapot.

☞ Answers on page 107

Review 1

Now let's see what you remember of the words you learnt in Units 1–5. There are six tests in this review. You could do them all in one session, or you could break them up and do them over a few days.

Step 1 Look at each group of words in the test to revise the spellings.

Step 2 Cover the four words up and test yourself (column 2). Try to do all four words in one go.

Step 3 Write your score out of 4 in the box. If you got any words wrong, go back and study them again.

Step 4 If possible, ask someone to test you on the words later—an hour or even a day later (column 3).

Test 1

Study	Test yourself	Test with another person
ant duck fox chicken	/4	/4
cow fly lion tiger	/4	/4
elephant animal crabs water	/4	/4
	Total score = out of 12	Total score = out of 12

Test 2

Study	Test yourself	Test with another person
sunny fish rocks towel	/4	/4
starfish beach ocean octopus	/4	/4
match jump skip beat	/4	/4
catch bounce team goal	/4	/4
	Total score = out of 16	Total score = out of 16

Test 3

Study	Test yourself	Test with another person
oval bathroom kitchen stairs	/4	/4
table chair food fridge	/4	/4
banana pear orange breakfast	/4	/4
dinner bread butter cheese	/4	/4
	Total score = out of 16	Total score = out of 16

Test 4

Jim has made some spelling mistakes in these sentences. Write the **bold** words correctly. An example has been done for you. Count your score when you have finished the test.

Jim's spelling mistakes	Correct words	Score ✓ ✗
Lines are big pussy cats.	Lions	
1 **Elefants** have long trunks.		
2 I read a story about a **duk**.		
3 Can you **sea** my dog?		
4 Don't **skipp** here, please.		
5 We toasted some **bred**.		
	Total score	/ 5

Test 5

Which words have been added together to make a new word? An example has been done for you. Count your score when you have finished the test.

Word	Made up of two words	Score ✓ ✗
bedroom	bed + room	
1 seagull		
2 teapot		
3 inside		
4 jellyfish		
5 bluebottle		
	Total score	/ 5

Test 6

There are three spelling mistakes in Meg's shopping list. Write the correct spelling in the spaces. Count your score when you have finished the test.

Answers	Score ✓ ✗
1	
2	
3	
	/ 3

☞ Answers on page 107

6 Myself

Quick fun

Unscramble the letters to make the words in the box.
The first one has been done for you.

hair	eyes
arms	legs
ears	head

1. rmsa 

2. raes ______________
3. hrai ______________
4. gles ______________
5. dahe ______________
6. yees ______________

Topic spelling list

Use the **LOOK-SAY-COVER-WRITE-SAY-CHECK** strategy to learn these words.

hair	head	face
ears	eyes	nose
tongue	mouth	neck
legs	knees	back
arms	hands	fingers
nails	feet	toes

Use this space to write out your topic words the first time. Use your own paper for extra practice.

Rewrite here those you had the most trouble with.

Spelling strategy

LOOK-SAY-COVER-WRITE-SAY-CHECK method

Choose six of the most challenging words from the **Topic Spelling list** and write them in Column 1 below. Then use the LOOK-SAY-COVER-WRITE-SAY-CHECK method to learn and practise their spellings.

1				
2				
3				
4				
5				
6				

Fill in the gaps

Choose words from the **Topic spelling list** to complete these sentences. The first one has been done for you.

1. I have rings on my ____fingers____.
2. My sister has her ______________ closed.
3. Her name is on the tip of my ______________.
4. Can you touch your ______________ yet?
5. My ______________ take size two shoes now.
6. Dad says my ______________ is always in the clouds.

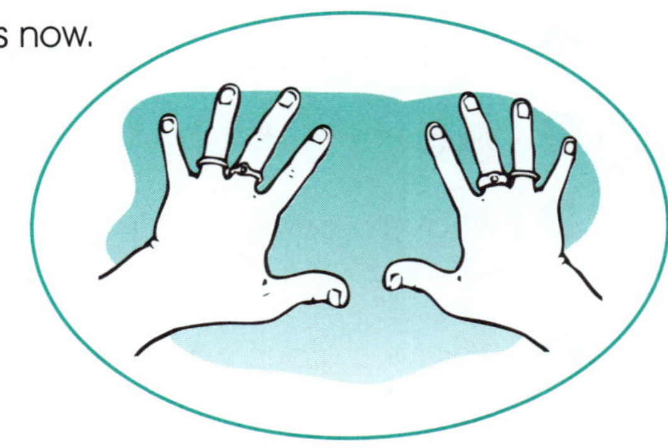

Tricky words

Some words are spelt and sound the same, but have different meanings.
For example: ***nails*** (thin pieces of metal with a sharp point) and ***nails*** (parts of your body on your fingers and toes).

Find the word from the **Topic spelling list** that has these different meanings.

1. **a** a leader
   b top part of the body

   The word is: ____________________

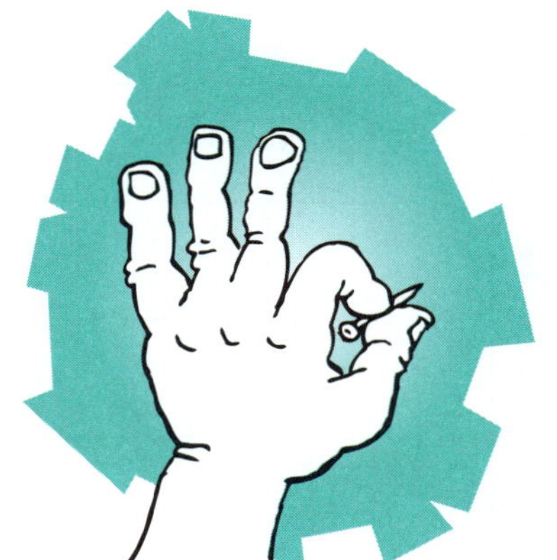

2. **a** pass something to someone
   b part of your body with fingers
   c set of cards in a game

   The word is: ____________________

3. **a** front part of a plane or rocket
   b something you breathe through

   The word is: ____________________

Looking at … the short vowel sound *a*

The short vowel ***a*** is like the ***a*** in *b**a**ck*. This sound is nearly always spelt with an ***a***. Many word families have this sound. For example: the ***at*** family (*c**at***, *m**at***, etc.), the ***ack*** family (*b**ack***, *p**ack***, etc.) and the ***and*** family (*b**and***, *h**and***, etc.).

Answer these questions with words that include the short vowel ***a*** and underline the short vowels in them. The first one has been done for you.

1. What do you wear on your head? hat
2. What do you play cricket with? ____________________
3. What is the opposite of white? ____________________
4. What is a short nail? ____________________
5. What are castles built from at the beach? ____________________
6. What is a group who play music together? ____________________

Proofreading

Find six spelling mistakes. Write the words correctly below. The first one has been done for you.

I am six years old. My hare is blak and I have blue i's. My leggs can run very fast. Today I tripped over and scraped my kne and two of my tos. Now I can't run as fast as before.

1. hair
2. ______________________
3. ______________________
4. ______________________
5. ______________________
6. ______________________

Vocabulary power

Look at this sentence: ***S**illy **S**am **s**kated **s**wiftly down the **s**lippery **s**treet.* See how the **s** sound is repeated. Repeating the same sound is called **alliteration**. This can make things sound scary, funny, sad, and so on.

Link words from column 1 with words beginning with the same sound in column 2. Say the words aloud to check you have the right pair. The first one has been done for you.

Column 1	Column 2
1 filthy	legs
2 knobbly	mouth
3 hairy	knees
4 lazy	toes
5 tippy	feet
6 motor	head

Read and learn

Read the text below. What do the words in **bold** mean?

My **plan** is to be on television one day. Mum says I have a **hope**. I like singing and dancing to any **kind** of music. What I would love **best** is to be in a musical with my friend. Then we could sing and dance **together**!

Circle the answer closest in meaning to the word in **bold**. The first one has been done for you.

1 **plan**	a map	b aim (circled)	c view
2 **hope**	a chance	b wish	c dream
3 **kind**	a group	b sort	c band
4 **best**	a less than other things	b more than other things	c same as other things
5 **together**	a with each other	b one after the other	c one before the other

Puzzle

The five labels on this person are in the wrong places. Label them in the right places on the empty picture.

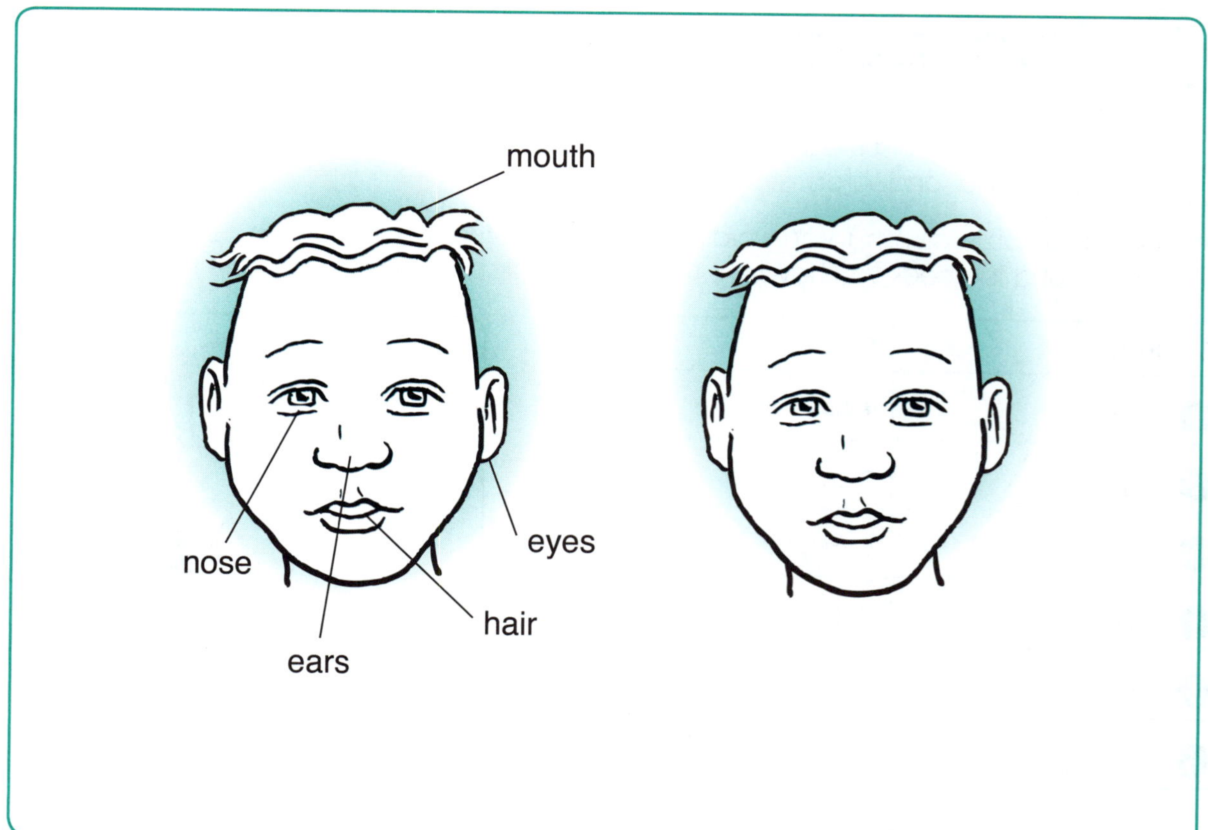

Your turn to write

Write your name or nickname down the page. Use each letter to add descriptive words about yourself.

For example:
SAM

Strong arms
Amazing singing voice
Many freckles

At the end of your description, add a picture of yourself.

My name ______________________

____
____
____
____
____
____
____
____
____

Reading for fun

✦ **I wondered why the baseball was getting bigger.**
❖ Then it hit me.

✦ **I'm glad I know sign language.**
❖ It's pretty handy.

✦ **I can run but not walk. Wherever I go, thoughts follow close behind. What am I?**
❖ ______________________

 ☞ Answers on pages 107–108

7 Families

Quick fun

Sort the words from the box into male and female.

aunt
brother
grandfather
sister
grandmother
uncle

Male	Female

Topic spelling list

Use the **LOOK-SAY-COVER-WRITE-SAY-CHECK** strategy to learn these words.

mum	mother	dad
father	brother	sister
grandmother	grandfather	aunt
uncle	cousin	boy
girl	son	daughter
parents	baby	children

Use this space to write out your topic words the first time. Use your own paper for extra practice.

Rewrite here those you had the most trouble with.

Spelling strategy

Learn a spelling rule: *ing* endings

The letters ***ing*** can be added to the end of a word to make a new word.

For example: *jump* → *jump**ing***.

Choose a verb from the box and add ***ing*** to complete these sentences.

play	heat
wear	blow
walk	talk

1. My aunt is ___walking___ to the shops.
2. Her sister is ______________ her new coat.
3. Are you ______________ cricket on Monday?
4. Mum is ______________ the baby's bottle.
5. The baby likes ______________ bubbles.
6. I am not ______________ about that.

Fill in the gaps

Choose words from the **Topic spelling list** to complete these sentences. The first one has been done for you.

1. She gave her ___mum___ a present for Mother's day.
2. My ______________ is my father's father.
3. We will have a new born ______________ in the house next year.
4. My ______________ is my mother's sister.
5. I have a sister but I don't have a ______________.
6. Only ______________ under ten years old could go.

Tricky words

The words ***son*** and ***sun*** sound the same but have different spellings. Think of a way to remember the difference.

For example: ***u*** stand ***u***nder the s***u***n.

Word	Meaning	Example
son	a male child	*My aunt has a new* ***son***.
sun	the round bright star you can see in the sky in the daytime	*The earth goes around the* ***sun***.

Complete these sentences:

1. Does the earth go around the s__n?
2. Her s__n turns six tomorrow.
3. It is too hot to be in the s__n.
4. I am my father's s__n.
5. Name a day of the week that has an ***un*** sound spelt ***un***.

   Answer: ___________________________

6. Name a day of the week that has an ***un*** sound spelt ***on***.

   Answer: ___________________________

Looking at … the short vowel sound *u*

You often hear the short vowel sound ***u*** in a word. It can be spelt with a ***u*** (e.g. *b**u**t*, *sh**u**t*) or with an ***o*** (e.g. *s**o**n*, *m**o**ney*).

Say each word aloud in the list below and then underline the letter that makes the short ***u*** sound. The first one has been done for you.

1. us
2. up
3. won
4. uncle
5. Monday
6. fun

Proofreading

Find five spelling mistakes and write the words correctly below. The first one has been done for you.

We are having a garage sail. Mum has asked everyone in the familly to give her things we don't need. My ant gave some books and my unkle gave an old clock. My little bruther wouldn't give mum anything.

1. sale
2. ______________
3. ______________
4. ______________
5. ______________

Vocabulary power

Your name begins with a ***capital letter***. This is because capital letters are used to name particular people.
For example: ***B****illy*, ***M****s* ***J****ones*. They are also used to begin a sentence.

Maggie forgot to use any capital letters in her story. Circle the seven words that need capital letters. Write them correctly for her on the lines below. The first one has been done for you.

(mrs) kent asked her granddaughter, suri, to stay with her. she has a cat called puss and a dog called bertie. suri says they had a very happy time together.

1. Mrs
2. ______________
3. ______________
4. ______________
5. ______________
6. ______________
7. ______________

Read and learn

Read the text below. What do the words in **bold** mean?

My dad is the **tallest** in our family. Can you **guess** who is the shortest? Yes—it's the baby. The second tallest is my brother who has **turned** twelve. He is taller than mum **already**. I come in **between** mum and my little sister.

Circle the answer closest in meaning to the word in **bold**. The first one has been done for you.

1	**tallest**	a least tall	b largest	c most tall
2	**guess**	a think	b follow	c ask
3	**turned**	a become	b twisted	c changed
4	**already**	a soon	b now	c today
5	**between**	a outside	b the middle of	c next to

Puzzle

Can you make at least six words out of the letters in the word ***father***? The first one has been done for you.

1 heat

2 ______

3 ______

4 ______

5 ______

6 ______

Your turn to write

Write a story about a very naughty baby. Name the baby and tell about one or two things the naughty baby does. What happens next? At the end of your story, draw a picture of the baby.

Check all the punctuation and spelling in your writing. Read your story to someone in your family or to a friend.

The very naughty baby

Reading for fun

Message from son to Dad
No mon
No fun
Your son

Message from Dad to son
That's sad
Too bad
Your Dad

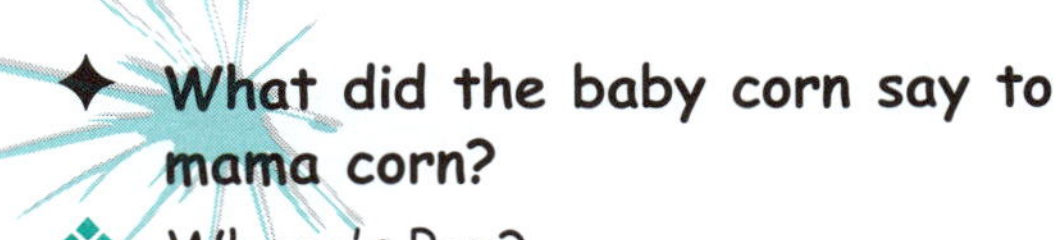

✦ **What did the baby corn say to the mama corn?**
❖ Where's Pop?

✦ **What's a baby's motto?**
❖ If at first you don't succeed, cry cry again!

☞ Answers on page 108

8 What are you wearing?

Quick fun

Match a word from the box to its picture. The first one has been done for you.

cap scarf jeans tie slippers pyjamas

1. pyjamas
2. ______
3. ______
4. ______
5. ______
6. ______

Topic spelling list

Use the **LOOK-SAY-COVER-WRITE-SAY-CHECK** strategy to learn these words.

dress	pants	hat
cap	clothes	coat
scarf	shoes	socks
t-shirt	washbag	shorts
swimmers	jeans	gloves
pyjamas	slippers	thongs

Use this space to write out your topic words the first time. Use your own paper for extra practice.

Rewrite here those you had the most trouble with.

Spelling strategy

Breaking words into syllables

Breaking a word into syllables can help you spell it. Remember to clap out the beats to find the syllables.

For example: ***sunhat*** has two syllables—***sun*** and ***hat***.

Break these words into syllables and circle their vowels. The first one has been done for you.

1. pyjamas py / ja / mas
2. sunhat ____________
3. raincoat ____________
4. nightgown ____________
5. trousers ____________

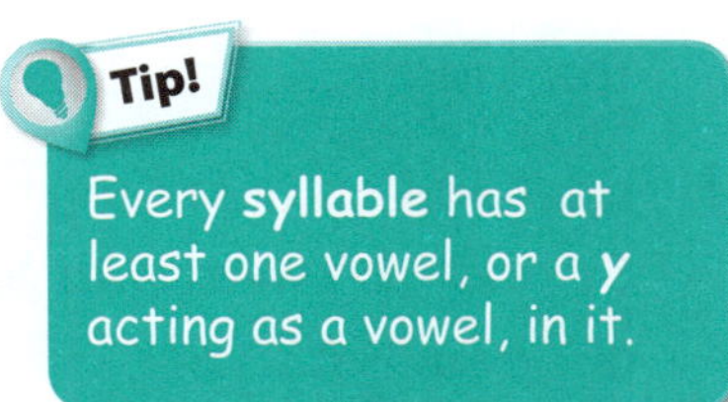

Fill in the gaps

Choose words from the **Topic spelling list** to complete these sentences. The first one has been done for you.

1. Is it too cold for shorts today?
2. Dad is ready for bed in his pyjamas and ____________.
3. She wore a ____________ around her neck.
4. We have to wear our school ____________ with our school shoes.
5. Sally wore her blue ____________ for her swimming lesson.
6. Mum wears ____________ in winter to keep her hands warm.

Tricky words

Some words are spelt the same and sound the same, but have different meanings. For example: ***shorts*** (short trousers) and ***shorts*** (short movies).

Find the word from the **Topic spelling list** that has these different meanings.

1. **a** breathes quickly in and out
   b clothing for the legs

   The word is: ______________________

2. **a** fur of an animal
   b clothing worn over other clothes
   c a layer of paint

   The word is: ______________________

Looking at … consonants

Letters in the alphabet that are not vowels (***a***, ***e***, ***i***, ***o*** and ***u***) are called **consonants**. There are 21 consonants in the alphabet, although sometimes the letter ***y*** acts as a vowel as well.

Write the consonants in the alphabet here.

____

____

____

How many vowels and consonants are there in these words? The first one has been done for you.

	Word	How many vowels (Vs)?	How many consonants (Cs)?
1	coat	2 Vs	2 Cs
2	dress		
3	socks		
4	clothes		
5	jeans		

Proofreading

Find six spelling mistakes and write the words correctly below. The first one has been done for you.

Mea can't gett her case to shut. Which cloths can she take out? She will need her pijamas. She'll also need her t-shirts and jeens. Perhaps she can leave out her slipers. She'll have to take out her cote too. That's better. Case closed!

1 get
2 ______
3 ______
4 ______
5 ______
6 ______

Vocabulary power

Adjectives add meaning to nouns. They describe things such as size and colour.

For example: The girl wore a ***long***, ***blue*** dress to the party.

Add an adjective describing colour to the nouns below. The first one has been done for you.

1 a red hat
2 a ______ coat
3 a ______ scarf
4 some ______ shoes

Add an adjective describing size to the nouns below. The first one has been done for you.

5 a large t-shirt
6 a ______ hat
7 some ______ socks
8 some ______ gloves

Read and learn

Read the text below. What do the words in **bold** mean?

Our class is putting on a play for Year Two **next** week. We **pretend** we live on a farm. I am a farmer. My **costume** is a green t-shirt, jeans and a hat with corks **dangling** from it. The farmer's wife wears a red t-shirt. There is **also** a cow in our play.

Circle the answer closest in meaning to the word in **bold**. The first one has been done for you.

1 **next**	a the one before	b this one	c the one after this one
2 **pretend**	a act as if	b tell	c say
3 **costume**	a what I dress up in	b swimmers	c suit
4 **dangling**	a dancing	b hanging	c twisting
5 **also**	a only	b because	c as well

Puzzle

Find and circle five differences between these two pictures.

Your turn to write

You are going on a beach holiday. There isn't much room in the car. You can take twelve items in a small case. Make a list of what to pack. At the end of your list, add a picture of you with your case.

Revise and edit your work. Check the spelling.

My list

Reading for fun

✦ **What do you get when you cross a cow and a goat?**

❖ A coat.

✦ **What's big and grey and protects you from the rain?**

❖ An umbrellaphant.

✦ **What did the baseball glove say to the baseball?**

❖ Catch you later.

✦ **What did the big furry hat say to the warm woolly scarf?**

❖ You hang around while I go on ahead.

☞ Answers on page 108

9 How many are there?

Quick fun

How many are there? Choose the correct number word from the box for your answer. The first one has been done for you.

two	one	three	four	six	five

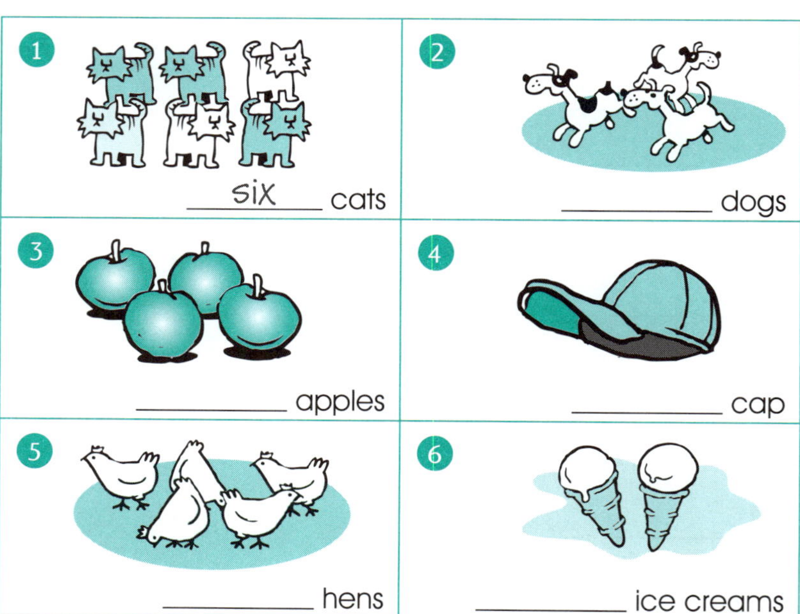

Topic spelling list

Use the **LOOK-SAY-COVER-WRITE-SAY-CHECK** strategy to learn these words.

some	lots	few
any	many	most
all	none	one
two	three	four
five	six	seven
eight	first	second

Use this space to write out your topic words the first time. Use your own paper for extra practice.

Rewrite here those you had the most trouble with.

Spelling strategy

Little words in big words

Some words have other words hidden inside them.

For example: ***one*** has the word ***on*** inside it (although the ***o*** in ***o****n* sounds different from the ***o*** in ***o****ne*). This can help you remember its spelling.

Find a word hidden inside these words. The first one has been done for you.

1. four ______our______
2. seven ____________
3. nine ____________
4. many ____________
5. none ____________
6. some ____________

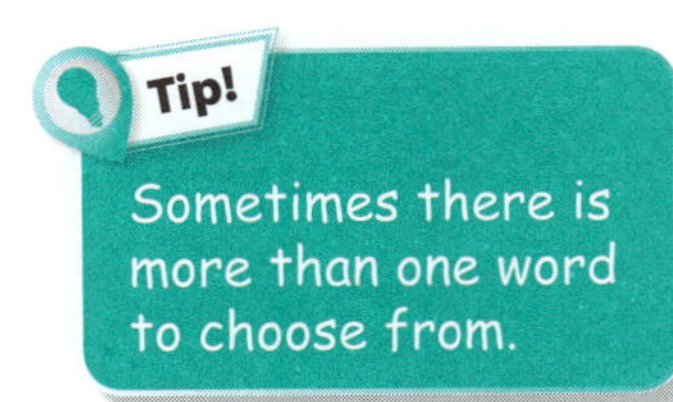

Fill in the gaps

Fill in the missing letters to spell the words from the **Topic spelling list**. The first one has been done for you.

1. t h r e _e_
2. f i __ __
3. m __ __ y
4. l __ t __
5. f e __
6. e i g __ __

Tricky words

The words ***some*** and ***sum*** sound the same but have different spellings. Think of a way to remember the difference.

For example: ***u*** do *s**u**ms*.

Word	Meaning	Example
some	not all	*She ate **some** of her dinner.*
sum	1 the whole amount	*I have a small **sum** of money saved up.*
	2 an exercise with numbers	*She did a **sum** on the whiteboard.*

Complete the sentence with the correct word (*some* or *sum*).

1. I left ______________ for you.
2. I got that ______________ wrong.
3. The ______________ of 1 + 1 = 2.
4. Will you give me ______________ of yours, please?

Looking at … consonant blends

Some consonants like to get together without a vowel between them. They are called **consonant blends**.

For example: the consonant ***s*** is often found with the consonant ***t*** as in ***st**eps*, or with ***p*** as in ***sp**ots*.

1. Underline examples of the consonant blend ***sp*** in this sentence.

   Six speedy wasps spun through space.

   How many did you find? ______________

2. Find and underline examples of the consonant blend ***st*** in this sentence.

   I stopped and stared at a most enormous elephant.
   It started to step up the stairs.

   How many did you find? ______________

Proofreading

Find six spelling mistakes. Write the words correctly below. The first one has been done for you.

The Olympic Games are held every for years. There are manny events such as runing and swimming. You can winn a gold medal if you come furst. I don't have anny hope of that.

1. four
2. ____________________
3. ____________________
4. ____________________
5. ____________________
6. ____________________

Vocabulary power

Choose an **adjective** from the box to complete these sentences. The first one has been done for you.

first	three
few	dozen
most	one

Tip!

Remember that **adjectives** add meaning to nouns. They can describe size and colour. They can also describe number.

1. I lost ____one____ thong.
2. I think ____________________ of the flowers were blue.
3. A ____________________ leaves fell from the tree.
4. We bought a ____________________ eggs.
5. There were ____________________ little pigs in the story.
6. He was the ____________________ man in space.

Read and learn

Read the text below. What do the words in **bold** mean?

We had to **guess** how many lollies were in the jar today. It cost a silver **coin** to make a guess. We were **raising** money for **sick** children in hospital. There looked to be a **great** number of lollies to me. I hope I win.

Circle the answer closest in meaning to the word in **bold**. The first one has been done for you.

1	**guess**	a add	(b decide)	c take away
2	**coin**	a money made of paper	b necklace	c money made of metal
3	**raising**	a collecting	b planting	c giving
4	**sick**	a thin	b unwell	c unhappy
5	**great**	a large	b wonderful	c good

Puzzle

			1		2			
	3		4				5	
6								

ACROSS

1. one plus one = ________
4. ten plus ten = ________
6. two plus two = ________

DOWN

2. three minus two = ________
3. a word that sounds the same as two but is spelt differently
4. two plus one = ________
5. five plus five = ________

Your turn to write

Write an account of the first time you did something all by yourself (e.g. rode a scooter, swam without floaties, tied your shoelaces or made your lunch). Explain what you did and how you did it. How did you feel? At the end of your account, add a picture of what you did.

Revise and edit your work. Check all the punctuation and spelling. Make a published copy for your teacher, parent or friend.

My first …

Reading for fun

Make up some actions for this well-known song using your ten fingers.

There were ten in the bed and the little one said,
"Roll over, roll over."
So they all rolled over and one fell out!
There were nine in the bed and the little one said,
"Roll over, roll over."
So they all rolled over and one fell out!
There were eight in the bed (and so on—seven, six, five, four, three, two)
Then—There was one in the bed and the little one said,
"I'm lonely …"

☞ Answers on page 109

10 Moving around

Quick fun

Write the words in the box in alphabetical order. The first one has been done for you.

walk	ride	drive
fly	sail	skateboard

1. drive
2.
3.
4.
5.
6.

Topic spelling list

Use the **LOOK-SAY-COVER-WRITE-SAY-CHECK** strategy to learn these words.

walk	ride	road
drive	fly	cruise
sail	arrive	leave
travel	track	stop
car	bus	train
plane	bike	skateboard

Use this space to write out your topic words the first time. Use your own paper for extra practice.

Rewrite here those you had the most trouble with.

Spelling strategy

Learn a spelling rule: more *ing* endings

You will remember that the letters ***ing*** can be added to the end of a word.

For example: *walk* → *walk**ing***; *sail* → *sail**ing***.

If the word ends in **e**, the **e** is dropped before adding ***ing***.

For example: *drive* → *driv**ing***.

Add an ***ing*** ending to these words. The first one has been done for you.

1. ride ______riding______
2. move ____________
3. arrive ____________
4. come ____________
5. leave ____________
6. dive ____________

Fill in the gaps

Choose words from the **Topic spelling list** to complete these sentences. The first one has been done for you.

1. Our family is flying in a ______plane______ to Fiji.
2. I rode my b____________ to school.
3. What time did you a____________ at school today?
4. Did you t____________ by car to the shops?
5. Does the bus s____________ here?
6. I travel by t____________ to school.

Tricky words

The words ***road*** and ***rode*** sound the same but have different spellings. Think of a way to remember the difference.

For example: ***road*** ends with a letter that goes up like a hill while ***rode*** ends with letters that go up and down like a bumpy ride.

Word	Meaning	Example
road	a track for cars, trucks and other vehicles to travel on	*The **road** goes from here to the park.*
rode	sat on something that moves	*I **rode** my horse to the fair.*

Cross out the incorrect word in these sentences.

1. They (road/rode) their bikes to the oval.
2. They (road/rode) along the (road/rode) to the shops.
3. The (road/rode) near our house is always busy.
4. She (road/rode) on the tram into the city.

Looking at … same sound, different spelling

The same sound can be spelt differently. The sound ***k***, for example, can be spelt with ***k*** (e.g. *wal**k***), **c** (e.g. ***c**ar*) or ***ck*** (e.g. *tra**ck***).

Circle the letters that make a ***k*** sound in these words. The first one has been done for you.

1. bike
2. rocket
3. come
4. kilometre
5. back

Now fill in the missing letters that make a ***k*** sound. The first one has been done for you.

6. We wal_k_ed down the path.
7. Is the car coming ba______?
8. Our taxi is ______oming soon.
9. I want some train tra______s for my train set.
10. I saw ______louds from the plane's window.
11. Would you like a ride on my s______ateboard?

Proofreading

Find five spelling mistakes. Write the words correctly below. The first one has been done for you.

In the holidays I stayed with my friend, Eliza. I caught the trane at the station and her family piked me up in their car. While I was there we went horse rideing with Eliza's dad. We went saileing once as well. It was a great holiday. I didn't want to leeve.

1. train
2. __________
3. __________
4. __________
5. __________

Vocabulary power

Remember that **adverbs** can tell how things are done.

For example: run ***quickly***, cruise ***slowly***. They often end in ***ly***.

Choose an adverb from the box to complete these sentences. The first one has been done for you.

sadly	badly	easily
softly	slowly	quickly

1. Run home quickly__________, please.
2. S__________, I lost the race.
3. He won the game e__________.
4. She drove s__________ along the track.
5. The wind blew s__________.
6. I fell and hurt myself b__________.

Read and learn

Read the text below. What do the words in **bold** mean?

It is my birthday tomorrow. I hope someone **remembers**. I **turn** six. I'd like a billy cart. I **doubt** anyone will give me that. I would **prefer** a computer game to a train set. But a bike would be really **great**.

Circle the answer closest in meaning to the word in **bold**. The first one has been done for you.

1 **remembers**	a forgets	b knows	c replies
2 **turn**	a become	b hit	c twist
3 **doubt**	a think	b don't think	c believe
4 **prefer**	a like	b like least	c like better
5 **great**	a good	b shiny	c clever

Puzzle

Can you make at least six words out of the letters in the word ***skateboard***? The first one has been done for you.

1 skate

2 ______________

3 ______________

4 ______________

5 ______________

6 ______________

Your turn to write

Explain how you get from home to school. Do you walk or catch a bus? Who goes with you? How long does it take? What do you pass? At the end of your explanation, add a map of your journey.

Revise and edit your work. Check all the punctuation and spelling. Make a published copy for your teacher, parent or friend.

My journey to school

Reading for fun

✦ **Why did the bus stop?**
❖ Because it saw the zebra crossing.

✦ **What's worse than raining cats and dogs?**
❖ Hailing taxis.

✦ **What did the train driver say to the frog?**
❖ Hop on.

☞ Answers on page 109

Review 2

Now let's see what you remember of the words you learnt in Units 6–10. There are six tests in this review. You could do them all in one session, or you could break them up and do them over a few days.

Step 1 Look at each group of words in the test to revise the spellings.

Step 2 Cover the five words up and test yourself (column 2). Try to do all five words in one go.

Step 3 Write your score out of 5 in the box. If you got any words wrong, go back and study them again.

Step 4 If possible, ask someone to test you on the words later—an hour or even a day later (column 3).

Test 1

Study	Test yourself	Test with another person
mouth knees hands toes hair	/5	/5
mother grandfather brother sister baby	/5	/5
pants shoes slippers jeans clothes	/5	/5
	Total score = out of 15	Total score = out of 15

Test 2

Study	Test yourself	Test with another person
some none eight first two	/5	/5
walk road drive track bike	/5	/5
feet tongue back fingers arms	/5	/5
running swimming driving going coming	/5	/5
	Total score = out of 20	Total score = out of 20

Test 3

Study	Test yourself	Test with another person
three four five six seven	/5	/5
plane train car skateboard bus	/5	/5
ears eyes see ocean beach	/5	/5
myself you few most many	/5	/5
	Total score = out of 20	Total score = out of 20

Test 4

Su Lin has made some spelling mistakes in these sentences. Write the **bold** words correctly. An example has been done for you. Count your score when you have finished the test.

Su Lin's spelling mistakes	Correct words	Score ✓ ✗
I hurt my **kneck**.	neck	
1 The **knail** on his toe was bleeding.		
2 My **grandmuther** gave me a hug.		
3 Please wash your **sox**.		
4 Are you **moveing** to the city?		
5 I'd love some new **cloths**.		
	Total score	/ 5

Test 5

There are ten missing **capital letters** in this text. Add them in the right places.

bob was running faster than ben. then he passed susan. he could hear his teacher, mr brown, cheering them all on. he heard sam, his dog, barking too. could he win the race?

Write your score when you have finished the test. /10

Test 6

Circle the word with the correct spelling.

For example: I can't (see/sea) her.

1. She (road/rode) her bike to school.
2. This (some/sum) is very hard.
3. I (ate/eight) a banana and a peach.
4. There are (none/nun) left.
5. Did you have (desert/dessert) last night?

Write your score when you have finished the test. /5

Answers on page 109

11 What season is it?

Quick fun

The four seasons are spring, summer, autumn and winter. Write the correct season's name under its picture.

1 ____________ 2 ____________

3 ____________ 4 ____________

Use this space to write out your topic words the first time. Use your own paper for extra practice.

Topic spelling list

Use the **LOOK-SAY-COVER-WRITE-SAY-CHECK** strategy to learn these words.

spring	summer	autumn
winter	weather	hot
warm	freeze	burn
rain	hail	numb
ice	snowman	cold
windy	cloudy	sunny

Rewrite here those you had the most trouble with.

Spelling strategy

Silent letters

Some words have silent letters. They disappear when you say the word aloud.

For example: **autumn** has a silent ***n***.

Say the underlined words aloud then circle the letter that is silent. The first one has been done for you.

1. The cold wind cut me like a knife.
2. Lambs are born in spring.
3. I know which season I like best.
4. My hands are numb from the cold.
5. Listen to the hail falling.
6. I saw a whale last summer.

Fill in the gaps

Choose words from the **Topic spelling list** to complete these sentences. The first one has been done for you.

1. Now that ___winter___ is here, I wear warm clothes.
2. The sky is very ______________ today.
3. Our water tank is full from the ______________.
4. I looked at the ______________ report on the web.
5. We sat by the fire to get ______________.
6. Our ______________ has melted.

Tricky words

Some words are spelt the same and sound the same, but have different meanings. Find the word from the **Topic spelling list** that has these different meanings.

1. a jump up suddenly

   b wire that jumps back into shape when stretched

   c a season that follows winter

   The word is: ______________________

2. a without any warmth

   b a sickness with a stuffy nose

   The word is: ______________________

3. a to put a sweet layer over a cake

   b water that has frozen

   The word is: ______________________

Looking at ... the long vowel sound *a*

You often find the long vowel sound ***a*** before a consonant + the letter **e**.

For example: *m**a**te*, *g**a**te* and *l**a**te*.

Think of five words containing the long vowel ***a*** that rhyme with *r**a**ce*. Circle the long vowel in each of your words. The first one has been done for you.

1. chase
2. ______________________
3. ______________________
4. ______________________
5. ______________________
6. ______________________

Proofreading

Find six spelling mistakes and write the words correctly below. The first one has been done for you.

Our family is fliing to the snow for a holliday. I have never scene snow before.

Mum said it could be freesing. I hope it won't be windie as well.

We are packing very warm cloths!

1. flying
2. ______
3. ______
4. ______
5. ______
6. ______

Vocabulary power

Apostrophes are punctuation marks that look like this **'**. They are used to show where letters are left out to make words shorter. These shorter words are called **contractions**.

Short form (contraction)	Long form
I'm	I am
you're	you (singular) are
he's, she's, it's	he is, she is, it is
we're	we are
you're	you (plural) are
they're	they are

Write these sentences without **apostrophes**. The first one has been done for you.

1. I'm cold. I am cold.
2. You're very hot. ______
3. It's too cold to swim today. ______
4. We're going to the snow. ______
5. They're at the beach. ______
6. She's at my house. ______

Read and learn

Read the text below. What do the words in **bold** mean?

If the flowers and trees are **budding**,

If the smell of blossom **wafts** through the air,

If there is less **chill** in the air,

If it's September the first.

Then I **know** spring has **sprung**!

Circle the answer closest in meaning to the word in **bold**. The first one has been done for you.

1 **budding**	a making friends	b forming little buds	c falling off
2 **wafts**	a floats	b waves	c sings
3 **chill**	a warmth	b cold	c calm
4 **know**	a am sure	b worry	c doubt
5 **sprung**	a gone	b been	c arrived

Puzzle

Hi Grandpa

I am co___ing to A___stralia to visit you soon. Dad say___ it will be hot there.

Will you take ___e fo___ a swim pleas___?

Love

Max

1 Max left out some of the letters from his message.
Fill in the missing letters and write them here: ________________

2 Unscramble the letters to find the name of a season. ________________

Your turn to write

a Choose a place to visit for a holiday. ______________________

b Choose a season to make your visit. ______________________

c Choose a person to send a postcard to. Write their name and address on the right of the postcard below. Write a message on the left about your holiday.

d Draw a picture for the front of your postcard. Write the name of the place in the picture.

60

To:

____

____

____

____

____

Reading for fun

✦ **What does a cloud wear under his raincoat?**

❖ Thunderwear.

✦ **When can three giant dinosaurs get under an umbrella and not get wet?**

❖ When it's not raining.

☞ Answers on pages 109–110

12 Where is it?

Quick fun

Harriet has lost her pen. Where did she put it? Unscramble these words to find out. The first one has been done for you.

under
on
in
beneath
near
inside

1. She didn't put it ni her desk. ___in___
2. She didn't put it rane her desk. ______
3. She didn't put it no her desk. ______
4. She didn't put it dnuer her desk. ______
5. She did put it diseni her desk. ______

Answer: Harriet put her pen ______ her desk.

Topic spelling list

Use the **LOOK-SAY-COVER-WRITE-SAY-CHECK** strategy to learn these words.

north	south	west
east	left	right
in	on	over
under	to	beneath
below	down	inside
off	up	near

Use this space to write out your topic words the first time. Use your own paper for extra practice.

______

Rewrite here those you had the most trouble with.

______

Spelling strategy

LOOK-SAY-COVER-WRITE-SAY-CHECK method

Choose six of the most challenging words from the **Topic Spelling list** and write them in Column 1 below. Then use the LOOK-SAY-COVER-WRITE-SAY-CHECK method to learn and practise their spellings.

1				
2				
3				
4				
5				
6				

Fill in the gaps

Using the clues that are there to help you, choose words from the **Topic spelling list** to complete these sentences. The first one has been done for you.

1. My friend lives _o_ v _e_ _r_ the road.
2. We had a picnic u ___ ___ ___ ___ the trees.
3. Her house is ___ e ___ ___ the river.
4. His hat peg is ___ ___ n ___ ___ ___ ___ mine.
5. Are you going ___ o school?
6. They ran ___ o ___ ___ the hill.

Tricky words

The words ***to***, ***too*** and ***two*** sound the same but have different meanings and spellings. Think of ways to remember the differences.
For example: think of *two* ***w****itches* to remind you that the number ***two*** has a ***w*** inside it.

Let the two **o**s in ***too*** remind you of more or extra. The smallest ***to*** does the hardest work. It goes with the base of all verbs (e.g. ***to*** run and ***to*** jump) and tells about moving towards (e.g. ***to*** the shops).

Word	Meaning	Example
to	**1** towards	*She went* ***to*** *the shops.*
	2 before a verb	*I want* ***to*** *come with her*
too	**1** as well	*Will you go* ***too****?*
	2 more than you need	*I ate* ***too*** *much dessert.*
two	the number after one	*There are* ***two*** *windows in my room.*

Test your memory by writing the correct word (*to*, *too* or *two*) in these sentences without looking back at the different meanings.

1. Jim is coming ________________.
2. May I have ________________ cupcakes, please?
3. My cat is ________________ fat.
4. Please take me ________________ the game.
5. Go ________________ bed at once!
6. It is after ________________ o'clock already.
7. You are ________________ tired ________________ stay up late.
8. I want ________________ of you ________________ come ________________!

Now check your work by looking back at the meanings.

Looking at … the short vowel sound *i*

You will often find the short vowel sound ***i*** at the beginning of a word such as *in* or between two consonants, as in *pin*.

Think of six three-letter words that rhyme with ***pin***. Circle the short vowel sound ***i*** in your words. The first one has been done for you.

1. b(i)n
2. ________________
3. ________________
4. ________________
5. ________________
6. ________________

Proofreading

Find six spelling mistakes. Write the words correctly below. The first one has been done for you.

I aksed Mark to come ofer after school today. I waited a long time four him. He said he had turned left instead of rite. Then he went west instead of eest. He was so glad too find my house at last.

1. asked
2. ________________
3. ________________
4. ________________
5. ________________
6. ________________

Vocabulary power

Prefixes are letters added to the beginning of a word to change its meaning.

For example: ***in*** + ***side*** = ***inside***.

Common prefixes include:

Prefix	**Meaning**
in	into
pre	before
sub	under
tri	three
un	not

Match a prefix from the table to the words below to make a new word. The first one has been done for you.

1. in + doors = indoors
2. ________ + marine = ________
3. ________ + angle = ________
4. ________ + school = ________
5. ________ + done = ________

Read and learn

Read the text below. What do the words in **bold** mean?

We are **travelling** by car to Canberra. Mum and Dad are in the front. I am **beside** my brother in the **back**. It is taking **forever** to get there. I **want** to read but I get car sick if I do.

Circle the answer closest in meaning to the word in **bold**. The first one has been done for you.

1	**travelling**	a (going)	b flying	c moving
2	**beside**	a behind	b next to	c on top of
3	**back**	a near the edge	b upside down	c behind the front
4	**forever**	a a long time	b some days	c many years
5	**want**	a am going to	b would like to	c shall

Puzzle

Can you help the wriggly worm find his way through the maze? Trace along the paths with your finger. When you find a way through mark it with a coloured pencil.

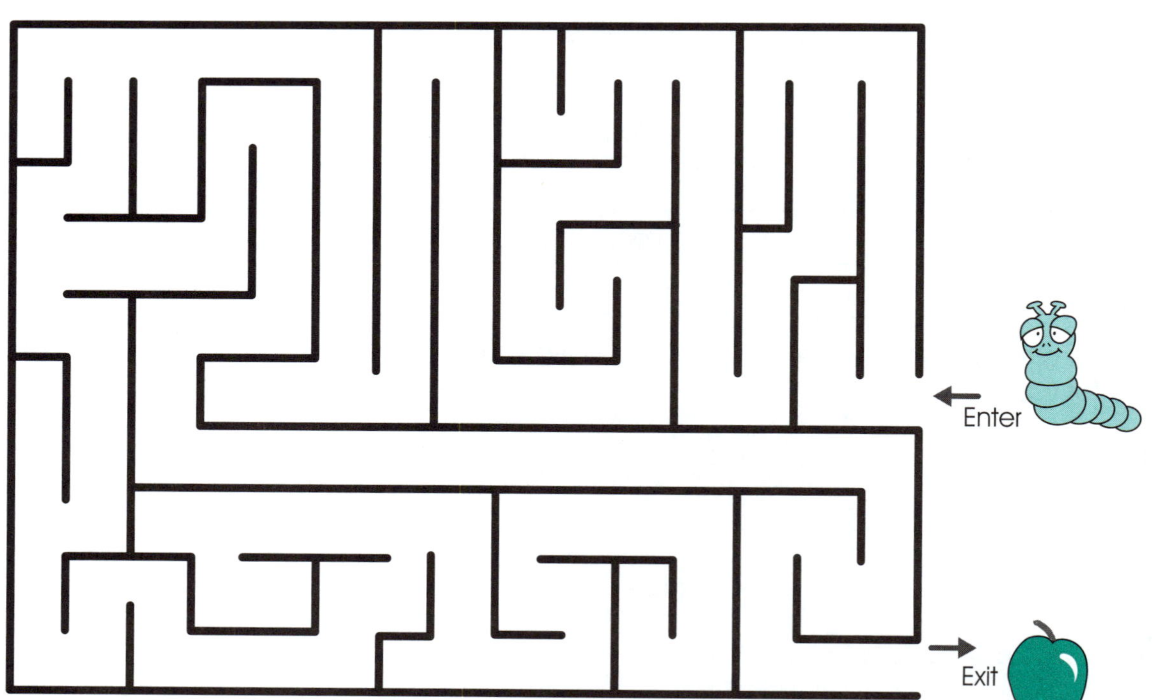

Your turn to write

Draw and label a map of your school. Show how to get from the front gate of your school to your classroom.

Reading for fun

✦ **What's the best way to remove paint from a chair?**

❖ Sit down before it is dry.

✦ **How do you get four elephants in a car?**

❖ Two in the front and two in the back.

✦ **What did the guide say to the man who pointed out some tiger tracks?**

❖ "You see where they go and I'll find out where they came from."

☞ Answers on page 110

13 How does my garden grow?

Quick fun

Unscramble the letters to make the word in the box. The first one has been done for you.

ground	shoots	roots	buds
sunlight	flower	leaves	

1. lignutsh ___sunlight___
2. sotor ________
3. olwfre ________
4. sdbu ________
5. dugrno ________
6. tosohs ________
7. seavle ________

Use this space to write out your topic words the first time. Use your own paper for extra practice.

Topic spelling list

Use the **LOOK-SAY-COVER-WRITE-SAY-CHECK** strategy to learn these words.

earth	sky	air
water	seeds	ground
root	shoot	bud
leaf	grow	plant
soil	sunlight	fruit
bush	flower	tree

Rewrite here those you had the most trouble with.

Spelling strategy

Little words in big words

Some words have other words hidden inside them.

For example: ***one*** has the word ***on*** inside it. This can help you remember its spelling.

Find a word hidden inside these words. The first one has been done for you.

1. earth ______ear, art______
2. water ____________________
3. ground ____________________
4. soil ____________________
5. bush ____________________
6. flower ____________________

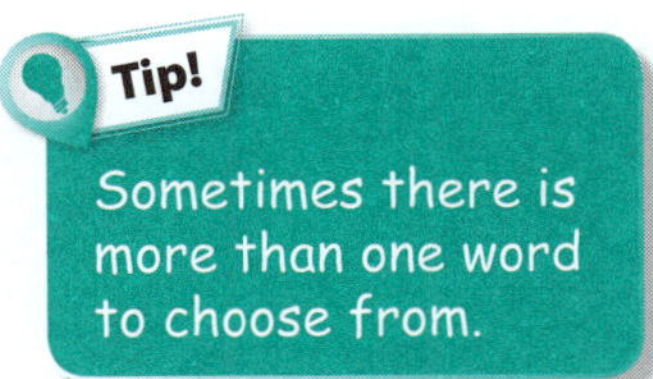

Fill in the gaps

Choose words from the **Topic spelling list** to complete these sentences. The first one has been done for you.

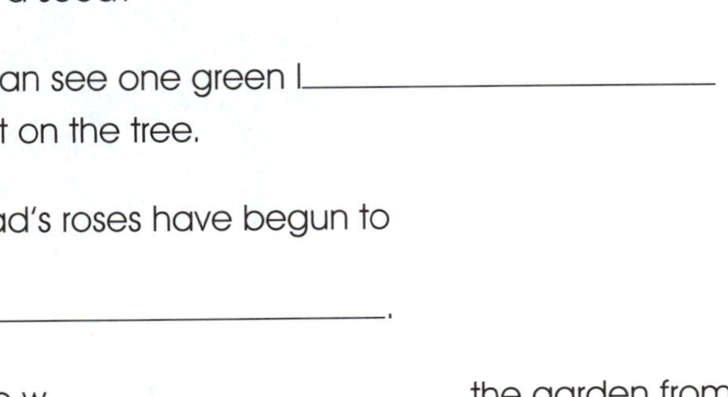

1. I love digging in the s<u>oil</u>____________________.
2. Did you p____________________ that sunflower as a seed?
3. I can see one green l____________________ left on the tree.
4. Dad's roses have begun to f____________________.
5. We w____________________ the garden from our water tank.
6. There is a new b____________________ on this lemon tree..

Tricky words

Most words ending with ***f*** add the letters **s** or **es** for their plurals.
For example: *cliff* → *cliff****s***.

But some words ending in ***f*** are a bit tricky. They change their ending to ***ves***.
For example: *calf* → *cal****ves***.

Choose a plural from the box and place it beside its singular form. The first one has been done for you.

halves
knives
shelves
thieves
elves
leaves

Singular	Plural
shelf	shelves
elf	
half	
leaf	
thief	
knife	

Looking at … vowel digraphs

When some vowels are side by side they make a single sound. For example: **ee** as in *I s****ee*** *a b****ee***; **oo** as in *S****oo****n you'll see the m****oo****n*.

Circle the vowel pair **ee** in words in these sentences. The first one has been done for you.

1. Thr(ee) of my roses have flowered.
2. You can plant the seeds here.
3. We ate lunch under that old tree.
4. The grass is as green as it has ever been.

Circle the vowel pair **oo** in words in these sentences.

5. We have a vegetable garden at school.
6. They grow food to sell at the market.
7. This plant has roots and shoots already!

Tip!

The ***ee*** or the ***oo*** can come anywhere in a word as long as the letters are together.

Proofreading

Find six spelling mistakes and write the words correctly below. The first one has been done for you.

I hop you'll pardon my gardon. It is ful of weads and thistles.

The roses have all died. The paths need sweping.

I think I've lost my green thum!

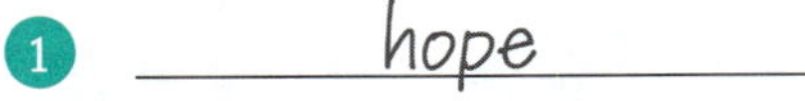

Vocabulary power

Suffixes are letters added to the end of a word to change its meaning.

For example: plant + ***ed*** = **planted**, plant + ***ing*** = **planting**.

Add a **suffix** to the underlined word in these sentences. The first one has been done for you.

1. She plant*ed*___ the roses yesterday.
2. Are you grow______ sunflowers there?
3. He water______ the garden with the new hose.
4. She is turn______ over the soil with a spade.
5. The leaves are blow______ in the wind.
6. He mow______ the grass so we could play there.

Read and learn

Read the text below. What do the words in **bold** mean?

We have a compost **heap** in our garden. My job is to add food **scraps** to it. My brother adds leaves and grass **clippings**. We **mulch** around our plants with the compost. This helps **prevent** weeds growing and feeds the plants.

Circle the answer closest in meaning to the word in **bold**. The first one has been done for you.

1	**heap**	a pile	b mess	c shed
2	**scraps**	a bags	b blocks	c small pieces
3	**clippings**	a cut off pieces	b clippers	c seeds
4	**mulch**	a dig up the soil	b cover the soil	c water the soil
5	**prevent**	a grow	b stop	c make

Puzzle

There are five **plural nouns** hiding in this puzzle. They name things that grow in the garden: leaves, seeds, plants, flowers and weeds. Draw a coloured line around each plural noun when you find it.

p	w	b	o	q	o	z	a
l	e	a	v	e	s	o	e
a	e	e	r	f	z	o	i
n	d	p	o	h	x	s	o
t	s	x	k	e	y	e	u
s	s	o	r	e	w	e	s
h	i	t	a	f	d	d	s
f	l	o	w	e	r	s	j

Your turn to write

Write a description of a secret garden. How does it look? What is in it? What happens there? At the end of your description, draw a picture of your secret garden.

Revise and edit your work. Check all the punctuation and spelling. Make a published copy for your teacher, parent or friend.

The secret garden

Reading for fun

✦ What did the nut say when it sneezed?
❖ Cashew!

✦ How do trees get on the Internet?
❖ They log in!

✦ The more of me you take, the more you leave behind. What am I?
❖

Answers on page 110

14 Making sounds

Quick fun

Use the words from the box to name the sounds below. The first one has been done for you.

whistle
whisper
buzz
neigh
moo

1. a very soft sound ______ *whisper*
2. a sound made by a bee ______
3. a sound made by a cow ______
4. a sound made by blowing through rounded lips ______
5. a sound made by a horse ______

Use this space to write out your topic words the first time. Use your own paper for extra practice.

Topic spelling list

Use the **LOOK-SAY-COVER-WRITE-SAY-CHECK** strategy to learn these words

scream	yell	whisper
whistle	rhyme	tune
chord	play	blow
cheer	clap	thud
cheep	moo	bark
neigh	hiss	buzz

Rewrite here those you had the most trouble with.

Spelling strategy

Memory tricks

You can remember how to spell a hard word with a memory trick.

For example, you can:

1 make up a funny sentence.

***R**ude **h**ens **y**ell **m**usic **e**ndlessly* could remind you how to spell the tricky word *rhyme*.

2 put words together that repeat a spelling pattern.

*I scr**ea**m for ice cr**ea**m* could remind you of the **ea** spelling pattern.

3 think of your own trick. The word ***whisper*** is difficult to spell. How could you remember its spelling?

Fill in the gaps

Choose words from the **Topic spelling list** to complete these sentences. The first one has been done for you.

1. She played the ____chord____ loudly on the piano.
2. I told my dog not to ____________.
3. She whistled a happy ____________.
4. The book fell with a loud ____________.
5. ____________ rhymes with kiss.
6. I am going to ____________ on our team at the match today.

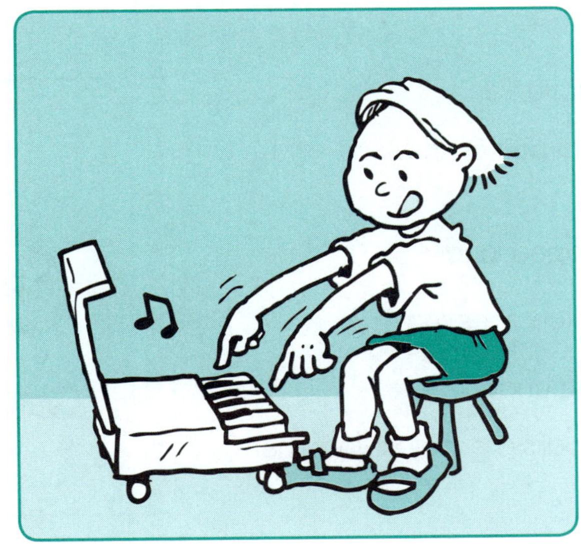

Tricky words

The words ***chord*** and ***cord*** sound the same but have different spellings and different meanings. Think of a way to remember the difference.

For example: ***choirs*** sing ***chords***.

Word	Meaning	Example
chord	notes played together	*I learned to play a **chord** on the piano.*
cord	1 string or rope	*You could tie that up with **cord**.*
	2 electrical cord	*That **cord** connects my computer.*

Complete the sentence with the correct spelling (*chord* or *cord*).

1. Play that ______________________ again, please.
2. Plug that ______________________ in here, please.
3. His spinal ______________________ has been hurt.
4. The music began with a loud ______________________.

Looking at … consonant digraphs

When some **consonants** are side by side they make a single sound.
For example: ***th*** as in ***th****is*, ***th****at* or ***th****e o****th****er* / ***ch*** as in ***Ch****itty* ***Ch****itty Bang Bang*.

Underline the **consonant pair *th*** in words in these sentences.
The first one has been done for you.

Tip! The ***th*** or ***ch*** can come anywhere in a word as long as the letters are together.

1. <u>Th</u>ey played <u>th</u>e an<u>th</u>em at <u>th</u>e concert.
2. That was a thrilling clap of thunder!
3. A thousand thanks!
4. This is our new theatre.

Underline the **consonant pair *ch*** in words in these sentences.

5. The chickens cheeped loudly.
6. Did you hear children cheering?
7. I have a child-sized chair.

How many consonant pairs are there altogether?

____

Proofreading

Find five spelling mistakes. Write the words correctly below. The first one has been done for you.

The animles wanted there dinner. First, the cows started mowing. That set off the dogs! They barcked very loudly. Then the horses began to nay. The noise made a deafening din.

1. animals
2. ____________
3. ____________
4. ____________
5. ____________

Vocabulary power

Sound words sound like, or imitate, the sound that is described.
For example: animal noises such as ***quack*** and ***purr***, or car noises such as ***honk*** or ***beep beep***.

Answer these questions with a **sound word** from the box.
The first one has been done for you.

splash	oink
ding dong	tick tock
gurgle	hiss

1. What sound does water make going down a drain? gurgle
2. What sound does a clock make? ____________
3. What sound does a pig make? ____________
4. What sound do waves make against the sand? ____________
5. What sound does a snake make? ____________
6. What sound do bells make? ____________

Read and learn

Read the text below. What do the words in **bold** mean?

> The didgeridoo is a **musical** instrument. It makes a very deep sound. Didgeridoos were **developed** by Aboriginal people at least 1500 years ago. **Today** didgeridoos are **often** about 1.2 metres long. They are rather **like** a long wooden trumpet.

Circle the answer closest in meaning to the word in **bold**. The first one has been done for you.

1 **musical**	a makes noise	b makes sound	c makes music (circled)
2 **developed**	a made	b played	c bought
3 **today**	a now	b in the past	c in the future
4 **often**	a sometimes	b always	c mostly
5 **like**	a different from	b the same as	c similar to

Puzzle

Work out the names of the musical instruments to complete this crossword.

■	1	■	■	■	■	■	2	■	■
3					■	■		■	■
■		■	■	■	■	■		■	■
■		■	4						
■		■	■	■	■	■		■	■
5								■	■
■		■	■	■	■	■		■	■
■	6				■	■		■	■
■		■	■	■	■	■	■	■	■
■		■	■	■	■	■	■	■	■

ACROSS

3 pi_____

4 tr_____

5 tri_____

6 dr_____

DOWN

1 didg_____

2 cla_____

Your turn to write

Write about your favourite sounds.

For example:

I love the sound of ... *seagulls squawking at the beach.*

I love to hear ... *my friend call hello when I get on the school bus.*

Revise and edit your work. Check all the punctuation and spelling. Make a published copy for your teacher, parent or friend.

My favourite sounds

I love the sound of ... ______________________

____

I love to hear ... ______________________

____

I love the sound of ... ______________________

____

I love to hear ... ______________________

____

I love the sound of ... ______________________

____

I love to hear ... ______________________

____

Reading for fun

✦ **What sound do porcupines make when they kiss?**

❖ Ouch!

✦ **What's orange and sounds like a parrot?**

❖ A carrot.

✦ **What do you call an owl with a deep voice?**

❖ A growl.

☞ Answers on pages 110–111

15 Flying things

Quick fun

Unscramble the letters to make the words in the box. The first one has been done for you.

helicopter	plane
kite	balloon
rocket	jet

1. tike _____kite_____
2. lloonba __________
3. tej __________
4. rtocke __________
5. tercoplehi __________
6. lepna __________

Topic spelling list

Use the **LOOK-SAY-COVER-WRITE-SAY-CHECK** strategy to learn these words.

aircraft	helicopter	jet
rocket	balloon	aeroplane
kite	bug	wasp
insect	fly	butterfly
bee	bird	eagle
kookaburra	magpie	owl

Use this space to write out your topic words the first time. Use your own paper for extra practice.

____

Rewrite here those you had the most trouble with.

____

Spelling strategy

Look-Say-Cover-Write-Say-Check method

Choose six of the most challenging words from the **Topic Spelling list** and write them in Column 1 below. Then use the LOOK-SAY-COVER-WRITE-SAY-CHECK method to learn and practise their spellings.

1				
2				
3				
4				
5				
6				

Fill in the gaps

The missing words are from the **Topic spelling list**. They name things that can fly by themselves. The first one has been done for you.

1. The ____eagle____ soared high in the sky.
2. The ______________ sat on the old gum tree.
3. A ______________ lives for a very short time.
4. A ______________ makes honey.
5. A bug is a kind of ______________.
6. He is a wise old ______________.

Tricky words

Did you know that ***flys*** is **not** a word? The plural of the insect, ***fly***, is spelt ***flies*** and the verb ***fly*** changes to ***flies*** (he, she or it ***flies***). Think of a way to help you remember the differences in meaning and spelling.

For example: see the letter patterns in these poems.

Squirt!
One fly,
then two fl**ie**s d**ie**.

Help!
I fl**y** in the sk**y**,
Superman fl**ie**s across the sk**ie**s.

Complete the sentence with the correct word (*fly* or *flies*).

1. There's a ______________ in my soup.
2. The ______________ are buzzing at the windows.
3. Superman ______________ again!
4. We are going to ______________ to Perth in a plane.

Looking at … the long vowel sound *i*

Many words that end with a long ***i*** sound are spelt with a ***y***.
For example: *I sp**y** a fl**y***.

Complete these sentences with a word ending in ***y***. The first one has been done for you.

1. That soil is too ______dry______.
2. The ______________ is filled with clouds today.
3. There are fruit trees in ______________ garden.
4. Fruit ______________ is a garden pest.
5. ______________ did you turn off the hose?
6. Put the watering can ______________ the tap.

Proofreading

Find six spelling mistakes. Write the words correctly below. The first one has been done for you.

Most insects can flye. They often have to sets of wings. They can whirl their wings manie times a second. Flying helps insects find food and escape from enemeis. My favourite insect is a butterfli. The insect I dislike most is a be.

1 fly

2 

3 

4 

5 

6 

Vocabulary power

Remember that **apostrophes** are used to show where letters have been left out.
For example: *I'm* (*I am*).

Apostrophes are also used with nouns to show ownership. Singular nouns add an apostrophe and an **s** (e.g. the *bird***'***s* nest, the *pilot***'***s* uniform). Plural nouns add an apostrophe after the **s** (e.g. *the birds***'** *nests, the pilots***'** *uniforms).*

Put the missing apostrophes in the correct place to show who owns what. The first one has been done for you.

1. a kookaburra's wing
2. an insects flight
3. an aeroplanes engine
4. a boys kite
5. bees hives
6. magpies babies
7. butterflies wings

Read and learn

Read the text below. What do the words in **bold** mean?

I saw a helicopter **rescue** a man yesterday. The man had fallen down a cliff. When the helicopter **finally** arrived, Dad said "I'm glad the **chopper** is here." It didn't take long for the helicopter to **airlift** the man to **safety**.

Circle the answer closest in meaning to the word in **bold**. The first one has been done for you.

1	**rescue**	a look at	b save (circled)	c follow
2	**finally**	a swiftly	b quickly	c at last
3	**chopper**	a helicopter	b axe	c chopping board
4	**airlift**	a help	b float	c transport
5	**safety**	a place away from danger	b place nearby	c a safe

Puzzle

Can you make at least six words out of the letters in the word ***helicopter***? The first one has been done for you.

1. pot
2. ____________
3. ____________
4. ____________
5. ____________
6. ____________
7. ____________
8. ____________

Your turn to write

Imagine you have a magic carpet for a day. Write a story about what happens, where you fly and what you see. At the end of your story, draw a picture of your magic carpet.

Revise and edit your work. Check all the punctuation and spelling. Make a published copy for your teacher, parent or friend.

The magic carpet

Reading for fun

- ✦ **Why did the fly fly?**
- ❖ Because the spider spied 'er.
- ✦ **How do fireflies start a race?**
- ❖ Ready, set, glow!
- ✦ **How do you make a baby sleep on a space ship?**
- ❖ You *rocket*.

☞ Answers on page 111

Review 3

Now let's see what you remember of the words you learnt in Units 11–15. There are six tests in this review. You could do them all in one session, or you could break them up and do them over a few days.

Step 1 Look at each group of words in the test to revise the spellings.

Step 2 Cover the five words up and test yourself (column 2). Try to do all five words in one go.

Step 3 Write your score out of 5 in the box. If you got any words wrong, go back and study them again.

Step 4 If possible, ask someone to test you on the words later—an hour or even a day later (column 3).

Test 1

Study	Test yourself	Test with another person
autumn winter freeze rain snowman	/5	/5
weather cold numb cloudy spring	/5	/5
south right left beneath over	/5	/5
	Total score = out of 15	Total score = out of 15

Test 2

Study	Test yourself	Test with another person
inside under near east below	/5	/5
earth sky leaves seeds trees	/5	/5
plant garden sunlight fruit grow	/5	/5
whisper whistle scream tune chord	/5	/5
	Total score = out of 20	Total score = out of 20

Test 3

Study	Test yourself	Test with another person
rhyme blow clap thud cheer	/5	/5
neigh hiss buzz cheep bark	/5	/5
helicopter rocket balloon insect kite	/5	/5
butterfly kookaburra magpie owl bird	/5	/5
	Total score = out of 20	Total score = out of 20

Test 4

Liam has made some spelling mistakes in these sentences. Write the **bold** words correctly. An example has been done for you. Count your score when you have finished the test.

Liam's spelling mistakes	Correct words	Score ✓ ✗
I do not like windy **wether**.	weather	
1 She put the present **beneeth** the tree.		
2 Look at that pretty patch of **sunlite**!		
3 I'd love to go up in an **aeroplan**.		
4 There are too many **flys** this summer.		
5 The **magpis** were singing very loudly.		
6 I saw an **eegle** flying high in the sky.		
	Total score	/ 6

Test 5

Read the text below. What do the words in **bold** mean?

I can see some **baby** birds in their nest. I watch them **sometimes** from my tree house. Their mother feeds them worms that are still **wriggling**. She **pokes** the worms down their throats. They **squawk** when she leaves them.

Circle the answer closest in meaning to the word in **bold**. Write your score when you have finished the test.

				Score ✓ ✗
1 **baby**	a very young	b little	c older	
2 **sometimes**	a never	b often	c now and then	
3 **wriggling**	a turning and twisting	b dead	c skipping	
4 **pokes**	a floats	b pushes hard	c tosses	
5 **squawk**	a sing	b screech loudly	c whistle	
			Total score	/5

Test 6

Circle the word with the correct spelling.

1 Did you hear that (screem/scream)?

2 You must (whisper/wisper) in this room.

3 Did you (see/sea) that octopus?

4 I saw a full moon last (night/nite).

5 There aren't many (leafs/leaves) left on the tree.

6 (Autum/Autumn) is nearly here.

Write your score when you have finished the test. /6

☞ Answers on page 111

Word list

about
aeroplane
air
aircraft
all
animal
ant
any
apple
arms
arrive
ate
aunt
autumn
baby
back
ball
balloon
banana
bark
bat
bathroom
beach
beans
beat
bedroom
bee
below
bench
bend
beneath
bike
bird
blow
boat
bounce
box
boy
bread
breakfast
brother
bud
bug
burn
bus
bush
butter
butterfly
buzz
cap
car
cat
catch
chair
cheep
cheer
cheese
chicken
children
chord
clap
clothes
cloudy
coat
cold
cousin
cow
crab
cricket
cruise
cup
dad
daughter
didgeridoo
dinner
diving
dog
down
dress
drive
duck
eagle
ears
earth
east
eggs
eight
elephant
eyes
face
father
feet
fence
few
fingers
first
fish
five
flies
flight
flower
fly
food
four
fox
freeze
fridge
fruit
garden
gate
girl
gloves
goal
grandfather
grandmother
ground
grow
hail
hair
hands
hat
have
head
helicopter
hen
high
hiss
honey
hop
hopping
hot
ice
in
insect
inside
jam
jeans
jet
jump
kangaroo

kitchen
kite
knees
kookaburra
leaf
leave
leaves
left
legs
line
lion
lots
lunch
magpie
many
match
meat
milk
moo
most
mother
mouth
mum
nails
near
neck
neigh
night
none
north
nose
numb
ocean
octopus
of
off
on
one
orange
oval
over
owl
pants
parents
path
pear
peas
plane
plant
plate
play
pyjamas
quickly
race
rain
ran
rhyme
ride
right
road
rocks
rocket
root
run
running
sail
sand
scarf
scream
sea
seat
second
see
seeds
seven
shell
shoes
shoot
shorts
sigh
sight
sister
six
skateboard
skip
sky
slippers
slowly
snowman
socks
soil
some
son
south
speak
spring
stairs
stare
starfish
stop
stove
summer
sun
sunlight
sunny
sunscreen
swim
swimmers
swimming
table
tea
team
them
thongs
three
thud
tiger
to
toes
tongue
too
towel
track
train
travel
tree
trumpet
t-shirt
tune
turn
two
uncle
under
up
walk
warm
washbag
wasp
water
waves
wear
weather
west
whisper
whistle
windy
winter
won
write
yell

Answers

1 Looking at animals (pages 2–7)

Quick fun (page 2)
2 ant **3** hen **4** lion **5** duck **6** bat

Fill in the gaps (page 3)
2 cow **3** elephant **4** duck **5** kangaroo **6** bat

Tricky words (page 4)
1 line **2** lion **3** lion **4** line

Looking at … rhyme (page 4)
1 If I had a rat
I'd not be fond of that.
If I had a pig
I wouldn't do a jig.
I think I'd like a fox
but it might chew my socks.
I'll settle for a duck
and hope it brings good luck.

2 a hen **b** cow **c** dog **d** fly **e** ant

Proofreading (page 5)
2 lions **3** tigers **4** kangaroos **5** elephants

Vocabulary power (page 5)

	Adult animal	Baby animal
1	bear	kid
2	dog	joey
3	chicken	pup
4	duck	cub
5	goat	duckling
6	kangaroo	chick

Read and learn (page 6)
2 c **3** c **4** b **5** b

Puzzle (page 6)
1 fox **2** pig **3** chick **4** bat **5** koala **6** dog **7** hen **8** cat
9 duck **10** kookaburra

2 At the beach (pages 8–13)

Quick fun (page 8)
2 shell **3** sun **4** waves **5** crabs **6** sand

Fill in the gaps (page 9)
2 crab **3** towel, sunscreen **4** waves **5** sand **6** fish

Tricky words (page 10)
1 a near **b** speak **c** bread **d** seat **e** wear
2 Answer: No

Looking at … syllables (page 10)
2 starfish—2 **3** boat—1 **4** rocks—1
5 ocean—2 **6** octopus—3 **7** shell—1

Proofreading (page 11)
2 today **3** towel **4** sunscreen **5** beach

Vocabulary power (page 11)
2 sun + screen **3** shell + fish **4** sea + gull **5** jelly + fish
6 blue + bottle **7** swim + suit **8** sand + castle

Read and learn (page 12)
2 b **3** a **4** c **5** c

Puzzle (page 12)

s	e	a	b	h	p	r	g
h	e	a	t	q	o	m	o
e	v	s	l	w	o	d	g
l	s	w	i	m	l	u	g
l	i	a	n	s	t	a	l
b	u	t	t	a	r	m	e
f	g	e	o	n	e	c	s
p	t	r	o	d	o	i	l

3 Sporting fun (pages 14–19)

Quick fun (page 14)
2 skip **3** ball **4** bounce **5** jump **6** hop

Spelling strategy (page 15)
2 at/cat **3** go **4** ounce **5** ace **6** an

Fill in the gaps (page 15)
2 race/beat **3** won **4** bend/jump **5** oval **6** Catch

Tricky words (page 16)
1 match **2** skip

Looking at … word families (page 16)
Answers could include:
crop, cop, flop, lop, mop, pop, plop, shop, stop, top, hop, chop, drop, clop, prop.

Proofreading (page 17)
2 duck 3 match 4 oval 5 catch

Vocabulary power (page 17)
2 quickly 3 loudly 4 angrily 5 slowly

Read and learn (page 18)
2 b 3 c 4 a 5 a

4 At home (pages 20–25)

Quick fun (page 20)
2 chair 3 stove 4 kitchen 5 plate 6 bedroom

Spelling strategy (page 21)
1 path

2 kitchen

3 table

Fill in the gaps (page 21)
2 table 3 garden 4 stairs 5 gate 6 fridge

Tricky words (page 22)
1 stare 2 stairs 3 stare 4 stairs 5 stare

Looking at ... plurals (page 22)
2 bedrooms 3 stoves 4 benches 5 paths 6 boxes

Proofreading (page 23)
2 kitchen 3 bedroom 4 garden 5 road

Vocabulary power (page 23)
2 dish + cloth 3 in + side 4 out + side 5 play + room
6 tea + pot 7 home + made 8 dish + washer

Read and learn (page 24)
2 a 3 b 4 b 5 a

Puzzle (page 24)
Answers could include:
room, do, be, boom, broom, dome, door, mob, moo, more

5 What's on the menu? (pages 26–31)

Quick fun (page 26)
2 butter 3 eggs 4 milk 5 orange 6 pear

Spelling strategy (page 27)
2 meat 3 breakfast 4 bread 5 beans 6 peas 7 tea

Fill in the gaps (page 27)
2 banana 3 butter 4 eggs/cheese 5 honey 6 apple

Tricky words (page 28)
1 pear 2 pear 3 pair 4 pair

Looking at ... vowels (page 28)
2 long 3 long 4 short 5 long 6 short

Proofreading (page 29)
2 meat 3 cheese 4 bananas 5 pears

Vocabulary power (page 29)
2 gobble 3 chew 4 munch 5 nibble

Read and learn (page 30)
2 a 3 c 4 c 5 b

Puzzle (page 30)

ACROSS	DOWN
2 lunch	1 dinner
4 milk	3 cheese
7 breakfast	5 beans
	6 tea

Reading for fun (page 31)
Answer: desserts

Review 1 (pages 32–35)

Test 4 (page 35)
1 Elephants 2 duck 3 see 4 skip 5 bread

Test 5 (page 35)
1 sea + gull 2 tea + pot 3 in + side 4 jelly + fish
5 blue + bottle

Test 6 (page 35)
1 butter 2 cheese 3 beans

6 Myself (pages 36–41)

Quick fun (page 36)
2 ears 3 hair 4 legs 5 head 6 eyes

Fill in the gaps (page 37)
2 eyes 3 tongue 4 toes 5 feet 6 head

Tricky words (page 38)
1 head 2 hand 3 nose

Looking at … the short vowel sound *a* (page 38)
2 bat 3 black 4 tack 5 sand 6 band

Proofreading (page 39)
2 black 3 eyes 4 legs 5 knee 6 toes

Vocabulary power (page 39)

	Column 1	Column 2
1	filthy	legs
2	knobbly	mouth
3	hairy	knees
4	lazy	toes
5	tippy	feet
6	motor	head

Read and learn (page 40)
2 a 3 b 4 b 5 a

Puzzle (page 40)

hair
eyes
ears
nose
mouth

Reading for fun (page 41)
Answer: a nose

7 Families (pages 42–47)

Quick fun (page 42)

Male	Female
brother	aunt
grandfather	sister
uncle	grandmother

Spelling strategy (page 43)
2 wearing 3 playing 4 heating 5 blowing 6 talking

Fill in the gaps (page 43)
2 grandfather 3 baby 4 aunt 5 brother 6 children

Tricky words (page 44)
1 sun 2 son 3 sun 4 son 5 Sunday 6 Monday

Looking at … the short vowel sound *u* (page 44)
2 up 3 won 4 uncle 5 Monday 6 fun

Proofreading (page 45)
2 family 3 aunt 4 uncle 5 brother

Vocabulary power (page 45)
Mrs Kent asked her granddaughter, Suri, to stay with her. She has a cat called Puss and a dog called Bertie. Suri says they had a very happy time together.

Read and learn (page 46)
2 a 3 a 4 b 5 b

Puzzle (page 46)
Answers could include:
at, fat, hat, rat, the, far, he, her, hear, heart

8 What are you wearing? (pages 48–53)

Quick fun (page 48)
2 tie 3 cap 4 scarf 5 slippers 6 jeans

Spelling strategy (page 49)
2 sun/hat 3 rain/coat 4 night/gown 5 trou/sers

Fill in the gaps (page 49)
2 slippers/socks 3 scarf 4 socks 5 swimmers/cap
6 gloves

Tricky words (page 50)
1 pants 2 coat

Looking at … consonants (page 50)
The consonants are: b c d f g h j k l m n p q r s t v w x y z
2 1 V, 4 Cs 3 1 V, 4 Cs 4 2 Vs, 5 Cs 5 2 Vs, 3 Cs

Proofreading (page 51)
2 clothes 3 pyjamas 4 jeans 5 slippers 6 coat

Vocabulary power (page 51)
Answers could include:
2 a blue coat 3 a yellow scarf 4 some black shoes
6 a small hat 7 some long socks 8 some tiny gloves

Read and learn (page 52)
2 a 3 a 4 b 5 c

Puzzle (page 52)
Differences are:
Dad's moustache
Mum's brooch
The top of the boy's hair
The girl's pointed collar
The lampshade's frill

9 How many are there? (pages 54–59)

Quick fun (page 54)
2 three dogs 3 four apples 4 one cap 5 five hens 6 two ice creams

Spelling strategy (page 55)
2 even/eve 3 in 4 man/a/an/any 5 no/on/one 6 so/me

Fill in the gaps (page 55)
2 five 3 many 4 lots 5 few 6 eight

Tricky words (page 56)
1 some 2 sum 3 sum 4 some

Looking at ... consonant blends (page 56)
1 Six speedy wasps spun through space. Total number: four
2 I stopped and stared at a most enormous elephant. It started to step up the stairs. Total number: six

Proofreading (page 57)
2 many 3 running 4 win 5 first 6 any

Vocabulary power (page 57)
2 most 3 few 4 dozen 5 three 6 first

Read and learn (page 58)
2 c 3 a 4 b 5 a

Puzzle (page 58)

ACROSS	DOWN
1 two	2 one
4 twenty	3 too
6 four	4 three
	5 ten

10 Moving around (pages 60–65)

Quick fun (page 60)
2 fly 3 ride 4 sail 5 skateboard 6 walk

Spelling strategy (page 61)
2 moving 3 arriving 4 coming 5 leaving 6 diving

Fill in the gaps (page 61)
2 bike 3 arrive 4 travel 5 stop 6 train

Tricky words (page 62)
1 rode 2 rode, road 3 road 4 rode

Looking at ... same sound, different spelling (page 62)
2 ro(ck)et 3 (c)ome 4 (k)ilometre 5 ba(ck)
7 Is the car coming back? 8 Our taxi is coming soon.
9 I want some train tracks for my train set.
10 I saw clouds from the plane's window.
11 Would you like a ride on my skateboard?

Proofreading (page 63)
2 picked 3 riding 4 sailing 5 leave

Vocabulary power (page 63)
2 Sadly 3 easily 4 slowly 5 softly 6 badly

Read and learn (page 64)
2 a 3 b 4 c 5 a

Puzzle (page 64)
Answers could include:
at, sat, bat, rat, bet, set, road, take, board, rob

Review 2 (pages 66–69)

Test 4 (page 69)
1 nail 2 grandmother 3 socks 4 moving 5 clothes

Test 5 (page 69)
Bob was running faster than Ben. Then he passed Susan. He could hear his teacher, Mr Brown, cheering them all on. He heard Sam, his dog, barking too. Could he win the race?

Test 6 (page 69)
1 (rode) 2 (sum) 3 (ate)
4 (none) 5 (dessert)

11 What season is it? (pages 70–75)

Quick fun (page 70)
1 autumn 2 spring 3 winter 4 summer

Spelling strategy (page 71)
2 Lam(b)s 3 (k)now 4 num(b)
5 lis(t)en 6 w(h)ale

Fill in the gaps (page 71)
2 cloudy 3 rain 4 weather 5 warm 6 snowman

Tricky words (page 72)
1 spring 2 cold 3 ice

Looking at ... the long vowel sound *a* (page 72)
Answers could include:
sp(a)ce f(a)ce b(a)se c(a)se (a)ce p(a)ce

Proofreading (page 73)
2 holiday 3 seen 4 freezing 5 windy 6 clothes

Vocabulary power (page 73)
2 You are very hot.
3 It is too cold to swim today.
4 We are going to the snow.
5 They are at the beach.
6 She is at my house.

Read and learn (page 74)
2 a **3** b **4** a **5** c

Puzzle (page 74)
1 m, u, s, m, r, e **2** summer

12 Where is it? (pages 76–81)

Quick fun (page 76)
2 near **3** on **4** under **5** inside
Answer: inside

Fill in the gaps (page 77)
2 under **3** near **4** beneath **5** to **6** down

Tricky words (page 78)
1 too **2** two **3** too **4** to **5** to **6** two **7** too, to **8** two, to, too

Looking at ... the short vowel sound *i* (page 78)
Answers could include:
din fin sin tin win

Proofreading (page 79)
2 over **3** for **4** right **5** east **6** to

Vocabulary power (page 79)
2 sub + marine = submarine
3 tri + angle = triangle
4 pre + school = preschool
5 un + done = undone

Read and learn (page 80)
2 b **3** c **4** a **5** b

Puzzle (page 80)
Maze solution:

13 How does my garden grow? (pages 82–87)

Quick fun (page 82)
1 sunlight **2** roots **3** flower **4** buds **5** ground **6** shoots
7 leaves

Spelling strategy (page 83)
2 at/ate **3** round **4** oil/so **5** bus/us **6** flow/low/lower

Fill in the gaps (page 83)
2 plant **3** leaf **4** flower **5** water **6** bud

Tricky words (page 84)

Singular	Plural
elf	elves
half	halves
leaf	leaves
thief	thieves
knife	knives

Looking at ... vowel digraphs (page 84)
2 seeds **3** tree **4** green, been
5 school **6** food **7** roots, shoots

Proofreading (page 85)
2 garden **3** full **4** weeds **5** sweeping **6** thumb

Vocabulary power (page 85)
2 growing **3** watered **4** turning **5** blowing **6** mowed

Read and learn (page 86)
2 c **3** a **4** b **5** b

Puzzle (page 86)

p	w	b	o	q	o	z	a
l	e	a	v	e	s	o	e
a	e	e	r	f	z	o	i
n	d	p	o	h	x	s	o
t	s	x	k	e	y	e	u
s	s	o	r	e	w	e	s
h	i	t	a	f	d	d	s
f	l	o	w	e	r	s	j

Reading for fun (page 87)
Answer: Footprints

14 Making sounds (pages 88–93)

Quick fun (page 88)
2 buzz **3** moo **4** whistle **5** neigh

Fill in the gaps (page 89)
2 bark **3** tune **4** thud **5** Hiss **6** cheer

Tricky words (page 90)
1 chord **2** cord **3** cord **4** chord

Looking at ... consonant digraphs (page 90)

2 That was a thrilling clap of thunder!
3 A thousand thanks!
4 This is our new theatre.
5 The chickens cheeped loudly.
6 Did you hear children cheering?
7 I have a child-sized chair.
Answer: 17

Proofreading (page 91)

2 their 3 mooing 4 barked 5 neigh

Vocabulary power (page 91)

2 tick tock 3 oink 4 splash 5 hiss 6 ding dong

Read and learn (page 92)

2 a 3 a 4 c 5 c

Puzzle (page 92)

ACROSS	DOWN
3 piano	1 didgeridoo
4 trumpet	2 clappers
5 triangle	
6 drum	

15 Flying things (pages 94–99)

Quick fun (page 94)

2 balloon 3 jet 4 rocket 5 helicopter 6 plane

Fill in the gaps (page 95)

2 kookaburra 3 butterfly 4 bee 5 insect 6 owl

Tricky words (page 96)

1 fly 2 flies 3 flies 4 fly

Looking at ... the long vowel sound *i* (page 96)

2 sky 3 my 4 fly 5 Why 6 by

Proofreading (page 97)

2 two 3 many 4 enemies 5 butterfly 6 bee

Vocabulary power (page 97)

2 an insect's flight
3 an aeroplane's engine
4 a boy's kite
5 bees' hives
6 magpies' babies
7 butterflies' wings.

Read and learn (page 98)

2 c 3 a 4 c 5 a

Puzzle (page 98)

Answers could include:
he, let, lit, lie, rice, rope, cop, cot, core

Review 3 (pages 100–103)

Test 4 (page 103)

1 beneath 2 sunlight 3 aeroplane 4 flies 5 magpies
6 eagle

Test 5 (page 103)

1 a 2 c 3 a 4 b 5 b

Test 6 (page 103)

1 (scream)	2 (whisper)
3 (see)	4 (night)
5 (leaves)	6 (Autumn)

Notes